Pocket Parasha

מגיד
MAGGID
Tzohar

Rabbi David Stav

Pocket PARASHA

Translated by Rabbi Avidan Freedman

Tzohar
Maggid Books

Pocket Parasha

First Edition, 2024

Maggid Books
An imprint of Koren Publishers Jerusalem Ltd.

POB 8531, New Milford, CT 06776-8531, USA
& POB 4044, Jerusalem 9104001, Israel
www.korenpub.com

The publication of this book was made possible
through the generous support of *The Jewish Book Trust.*

ISBN 978-1-59264-678-4, *hardcover*

Printed and Bound in Turkey

Dedicated in loving memory
of our dear sons and brothers

Jonathan Theodore Lax, ז״ל
Ethan James Lax, ז״ל

לעילוי נשמת

יונתן טוביה בן מרדכי ז״ל
איתן אליעזר בן מרדכי ז״ל

נְדִיבֵי לֵב וְטוֹבֵי עַיִן אֲשֶׁר נָשְׂאוּ חֵן בְּעֵינֵי הַכֹּל

Michael and Marsha Lax
Amanda and Akiva Blumenthal
Rebecca and Rami Laifer

Contents

Exodus

Leviticus

Numbers

Deuteronomy

Special Parashot

Introduction

A few years ago, when I was asked to write a weekly column on *parashat hashavua* for the *Israel Hayom* daily, I asked myself: What can my writing contribute? Do we lack commentaries and commentators? What can I add, when bookshelves are bowing under the weight of the writings of the sages throughout the generations, who continually shed new light on the Torah? Yet another concern nagged at me as well. Perhaps this would be just one more column that the average reader prefers to skip on their way to other topics. But in the end, I decided that one of the more significant challenges of our time is to transmit the Torah to a generation that does not always fully appreciate it, and can even be quite distant from it, on account of differences in language and culture. Perhaps, then, my goal with this column is not that of the classic commentator, but as a sort of mediator who bridges the gap between what happens in the text and what is happening within us, in contemporary Israeli society. I thought that perhaps it would be worthwhile to convey to readers, who do not necessarily find themselves in the synagogue, something of my own experience of the reading of the Torah, some of the melody heard in the sanctuary as the reader chants the verses of the Torah.

Writing a weekly column, in a widely distributed newspaper, that seeks to be relevant and to find connections within the *parasha* to what is going on in contemporary Israeli society is fundamentally different than a commentary that aims to offer a coherent interpretation of the Torah, that aspires to connect to the eternity embedded within the text, and to transcend time and space. The differences between these two styles of writing become even more significant when trying to make the spirit of the verses accessible to readers who are not used to close analysis of ancient philosophical texts. The classic commentator – as opposed to this writer – wrote primarily for a captive audience, thirsty to learn, fully engaged in the desire to deepen its understanding of the verses. Furthermore, the reasons that justify writing for a newspaper, that fundamentally deals with the here and the now, do not necessarily suffice to justify turning these articles into another book in the library of Jewish thought, which by its nature has a stamp of eternity.

Nevertheless, it became apparent that many good people were interested in the ideas that emerged from this writing, including students of Torah and Torah scholars, along with people who do not study Torah regularly, and are even quite far removed from it. And so, we thought it would be proper to collect these columns in a book that could offer a comprehensive approach to connecting the Jewish people's eternal Torah to the contemporary challenges of Israeli society.

We cannot end this introduction before thanking several people. My profound thanks to the Lax, Blumenthal, and Laifer families for their support of this book in particular and Tzohar in general. May the memory of Jonathan Lax and Ethan Lax be a blessing. Thanks to Amos Regev and Gonen Ginat from *Israel Hayom,* who placed their confidence in me and allowed me to write in the paper that they edit. Rabbi Avidan Freedman did a wonderful job of translating my prose into English. Thank you to Matthew Miller, Reuven Ziegler, Gila Fine and the staff of Maggid Books for their work on the original Hebrew edition of this book, as well as to David Silverstein, Yoel Finkelman, Nechama Unterman, and Esther Shafier who spared no effort in ensuring that this work be published in the most worthy form possible.

David Stav

POCKET

Genesis

בראשית

Bereshit

It is for good reason that Genesis, the first book of the Torah, is called *Bereshit*, "In the beginning," and that this is also the name of the very first *parasha*. The name carries with it an air of renewal and innovation. Of course, the book starts with the story of the beginning of the world's creation, but for the community of Torah learners, it means much more than that. It brings with it an exciting, refreshing message: We are all starting to learn "from the beginning," the story can always be read anew, and new audiences can always join those who study and contemplate the Torah. In short – we start again, "from the beginning."

Any person who wants to seriously engage in learning Torah must consider the question: What precisely is "Torah"? Everyone knows that it is a book dictated to Moses by God over three thousand years ago. But beyond these chronological details, we seek to understand the nature and purpose of this text. Is it a book of laws and mitzvot, or perhaps a book of history containing fascinating stories of the world in general, and the Jewish world in particular?

The greatest of all Torah commentators, Rashi, begins his commentary on the Torah with this very question. "The Torah should have begun with 'And this month will be for you,' which is the first mitzva that Israel was commanded. What is the reason that it began 'In the beginning'?" Rashi's latent assumption is that the Torah is a book of mitzvot and laws. If so, the Torah should have begun with the first mitzva that the Jewish people were commanded while leaving Egypt. Why did the Torah choose to begin with the story of the creation of the world, and all the other historical events that surround the establishment of the Jewish nation?

Rashi offers an answer whose depth needs to be fully understood. "Because 'He has declared to His people the power of His works, in giving them the heritage of the nations' that if the nations of the world should say: 'You are robbers, for you conquered the land of the seven nations,' they can respond: 'All the land belongs to God.'" There seems to be no clear connection between the question and the answer. The question assumed that the Torah is a book of laws, and the answer suggests that we need to provide a response to the nations and to explain to them what we are doing here, in the Land of Israel. It's a nice idea, but what does it have to do with the Torah, which is fundamentally a book of laws? If we need a document that defends us against the nations' claims, then a separate one could be drawn up! Why put this in the Torah?

We could answer that the Torah, indeed, is a book of laws, but, for particular reasons, it began with a number of stories to satisfy peripheral needs. In this case, the Torah strays from its real purpose so that the nations will not accuse us of having stolen the Land of Israel from the Canaanite peoples, to tell us that, indeed, the land is ours, and that we are not robbers.

But perhaps we can suggest an entirely different answer. The Torah is not only a book of mitzvot, as many tend to think. Its name does come from the word "*horaa*," meaning "teaching," but the mitzvot are only one part of what it is coming to teach. Another part, no less important, is to teach us about God's actions in creating the world. The truth is that one who inspects the five books of the Torah will see that for the most part, they are not discussing the mitzvot, but the story of God's actions in this world. This is meant to lead us to the insight that despite our sense that we run the world, in truth, this palace does have an owner. By reading the first stories of creation, and the stories that come afterward, we are meant to internalize that the world has meaning and content; there is a leader and there is a purpose, there is a direction and intention to the world. Mitzvot are one of the expressions of this idea, but not the only one. Along with the mitzvot, we need to learn the world of values and ethics, reward and punishment for doing good and evil, sensitivity to one who is other and different, both individuals and collectives. An entire world of divine values is developed by studying God's way in leading the world. The book of Genesis is the first book that seeks to tell us the story of the world in a way that will provide us with meaning and help us understand our role in this world.

Noaḥ

Parashat Noaḥ, the second *parasha* of the book of Genesis, contains some of the most important and fundamental stories relating to human history. To summarize it in modern terms, we could say that the vision failed, and that the great dream of a utopian world shattered to pieces. God brings a flood, almost completely destroying His world.

Let's take a step back to review the previous *parasha*, *Bereshit*. God creates a near-perfect world of flora and fauna, places man at its center, and gives him the power to rule over all of creation. Initially, man rebels against God's command with a relatively minor act, by eating from the forbidden fruit of the Tree of Knowledge. The situation continues to deterio-rate, as Cain, Adam's firstborn son, kills his younger brother

Abel. In both of these cases, God punished individuals for their actions. But at the end of the *parasha*, we witness a further deterioration: "And the Lord saw that the wickedness of man was great in the earth, and that every imagination of the thoughts of his heart was only evil continually" (6:5). This verse speaks not of an individual who rebels against his Creator, but of all of humanity that constantly thinks and commits evil – the very opposite of God's will. In this situation, local punishment cannot suffice. Something drastic is called for, and thus the path is paved for the decision: "I will erase My creation, humankind, from the face of the earth" (6:7). God wants to annihilate His world. There is only one man who finds favor in His eyes, Noah. "And Noah found favor in God's eyes" (6:8). Thus ends the previous week's *parasha*. This week, we continue to follow the events. What will God do to a world that is wholly sinful, in which only one person does good? The proposed solution is to save that man by means of an ark; he will enter it, and the rest of the world will be destroyed in a flood. At the end of the story, after leaving the ark, Noah offers a sacrifice, at which point God informs him that He will never again destroy the world on account of humankind's sins: "For the imagination of man's heart is evil from his youth" (8:21).

These words raise a perplexing question. Didn't God

already know this beforehand? Did we not read, before the flood, that "every imagination of the thoughts of his heart was only evil continually"? What has changed?

A careful reading suggests that we pay attention to the unique phrase "the imagination of man's heart is evil from his youth." This phrase reflects a common reality among adolescents, perhaps, but one that can be repaired and directed. This isn't a fatalistic decree to which the human race is irredeemably condemned, without any capacity for improvement. Moreover, while this energy can bring forth great evil, it can also be directed in constructive ways.

What caused God to alter (as it were) His conception of the situation? It would seem that Noah's sacrifice was the deciding factor.

Perhaps this *parasha* comes to teach us of the power of the individual, of a single, simple person. At the beginning of the story, we hear of Noah who was good and righteous, but whose actions had no effect on his surroundings. He followed his path of righteousness, while the world followed its path of wickedness, and therefore, his behavior could not save a world full of corruption, violence, and sexual impropriety. But from the moment that Noah offered a sacrifice, affirming his faith in God and his belief in His values, God saw that man, while capable of great evil, can also do good, that he does not need to succumb to human evil. As long as even a few people will take responsibility for their lives, and the lives of those who surround them, the world can continue to exist. A famous tale tells of thirty-six hidden righteous people in whose merit the world exists. This legend expresses society's need to base itself on individuals who place the world's well-being before their own personal good. A person is tested by his ability to stand up to outside pressure, and to say that he is willing to cling to his beliefs and fight for them; in this way he can save the entire world.

Lekh Lekha

The main character in *Parashat Lekh Lekha* is Abraham, the father of the Jewish nation. Abraham is commanded to leave his birthplace, Ur of the Chaldees, and to go to the Land of Israel. He immigrates to Israel and there is forced to confront the difficulties that typically face new immigrants in their new homes: acculturation to new people, financial difficulties, famine, and the like. In contrast, the hero of the previous *parasha* was Noah, who had to face a corrupted world that was destroyed, and then to build a new world after the flood. A quick comparison between the biographies of the two figures reveals a fascinating difference. At the time of his birth, we are told that Noah will comfort the world, later he is called a "righteous and whole-hearted man" (6:9), and above all, we are told that he found favor in God's eyes. About Abraham, nothing similar is said. We know who his father was; his two brothers, Haran and Nahor, are also mentioned, but that is all. And then, out of the blue, God says to Abraham: "Go to another place, that I will show you. Leave your comfortable, familiar house for an unknown destination." We do not find a single word in the verses giving us even the slightest hint as to Abraham's personality, his character traits, or the like. We heard many stories about Abraham in kindergarten and grade school. One described Abraham wandering the world and yearning to meet its creator. Another told of the child Abraham who breaks the idols that his father sells, and a third story told of Abraham being cast into a fiery furnace on account of his faith and surviving. What all these stories have in common is that not a single one of them appears explicitly in the Torah.

All of this begs the question: Why? Why is it that what the Torah finds significant to tell us regarding Noah and his actions is not even hinted at when it comes to Abraham? Even the reason that Abraham is commanded to leave his home and travel to another land is not mentioned. In contrast to all of the events of the flood and the building of the ark, which are explained in great detail, fundamental questions about Abraham, his being chosen as the father of the nation and his immigration to Israel, are not explained at all. Why not?

Perhaps the Torah is seeking to convey an important

message. Over the course of Jewish history, many different and varying traits will characterize the nation's identity. For some of its existence, faith in God and commitment to His mitzvot will define this identity. In other periods, it will be the national elements that will be central. The Rambam saw the traits of humility, shame, and kindness as the defining characteristics of the Jew, going so far as to maintain in his halakhic writings that a person who is brazen should be checked as to whether they are truly Jewish. (Some later rabbis claimed that if we were to accept the Rambam's standards, we would not be able to marry, because brazenness has become so prevalent in later generations.) Had the Torah said that Abraham was chosen for this or that trait or action, that could have formed the basis of a position that claims that in order to be considered Jewish, it is enough to have such a trait or to do such an action. This is what the Torah wanted to prevent. The same is true for the reasons that he moved to Israel: We are here not because this country is better than others in any particular area, but because it is our land, period. It is reminiscent of what Israel's former prime minister Yitzhak Shamir said, humorously, but in complete seriousness: "Why Israel? Just because!" The Torah wants to emphasize that once Abraham was chosen (and certainly there were good reasons for this, as will become clear later), the fact that the Jewish people exist was established, and anyone who belongs to it is invited to dedicate their energies and abilities, and to contribute to its building.

Another interesting phenomenon that we also find in this *parasha* is the mitzva of circumcision commanded to Abraham. This is not one of the most logical mitzvot, to say the least; it involves physically harming a child's body, and it is difficult to explain its rationale. But nonetheless, this is a commandment that most of the nation fulfills to this day, including those who are not scrupulous regarding every mitzva. It could be that this is another reflection of the same idea. Not everything needs an explanation and a reason. I belong to a family because I am a part of it, for better or for worse, and my family has certain customs. I may not love everything about it all the time, and at times there are family members who run away. But someone who decides to remain a part of the family (or part of the Jewish people) does so with their heart and soul, even when its practices are not always understood or comfortable. To be a Jew is to live a life with a great deal of content and significance, even if we do not understand the fundamental reasons for its practices.

Vayera

The story at the beginning of this *parasha* offers an expansive glimpse into the way of life in Scriptural times. Abraham sits at the entrance of his tent at the peak of an intense heatwave of the type that is common in our region. According to the Sages, he was recuperating for a few days after his circumcision at the age of ninety-nine. But then he sees three strange men from afar (nomadic idol worshippers, according to one interpretation). Abraham, despite his pain, runs to them and insists that they come into his tent, wash up, rest, and eat something. And then, after they finish eating, there is a plot twist: we suddenly understand that these three men are God's messengers who have come to announce the birth of Isaac.

These would seem to be two stories that are fundamentally not connected: The first reflects Abraham's powerful love for humankind and his desire to do good for others. Despite his age and stature, he does not deem it beneath his dignity to bother himself with hosting unknown nomads. Moreover, Abraham had rejected the idol worship that was practiced in his day and chosen to worship the God of Israel. Nevertheless, he was willing to host anyone in need, without regard to their religion or beliefs, even if his guest seems to be an idol worshipper who worships the dust of his feet, as one of the midrashim suggests. In the second story, which immediately follows the first, we read of the angels telling Abraham that he will have a son in the coming year.

Couldn't Abraham have been informed about his son's birth without us being told of his kindness of hosting guests? The decision about the birth of Isaac was already conveyed to Abraham in the previous *parasha*. Why, then, does the Torah decide to connect these two stories?

Hakhnasat orḥim, hosting guests, is one of the most important values in the Jewish people's tradition of acts of kindness. Sometimes, we mistakenly think that this commandment's time has passed – that it is no longer relevant. In the olden days, when people were poor, and journeys treacherous, anyone who traveled from one city to another left their home for a long period of time and was in dire need of the generosity of their hosts. In modern times, in an era of prosperity, with rapid transit and hotels, some suggest that this practice has almost no value or meaning. But in fact, the very opposite is true. The reality in the Western world in general, and in Israel, as an immigrant-absorbing country in particular, creates an ever-growing estrangement between a person and their environment, and this even impacts a person's relationships with their close neighbors. *Hakhnasat orḥim* may be even more important and critical for us. Perhaps we should be dedicating more attention and awareness to it, and the sooner the better.

Over the course of two decades, from 1990 to 2010, Israel absorbed more than one million new immigrants. Many of them acclimated well, but others still get lost in the thicket of Israeli bureaucracy and society. More than once, I've met immigrants from the United States or the former Soviet Union who are surprised and upset that none of their Israeli neighbors ever invited them over for a Shabbat meal. They, who had made sure to host every Israeli who came and visited them, find themselves distanced, against their will, from the lively Israeli social world. This isn't, God forbid, the result of miserliness. We just have a hard time leaving our own Israeli bubble to make room, even for one evening, for a family that comes from a different culture, a different style of life, and a way of speaking unfamiliar to us. This is true not only regarding new immigrants, but even of hosting anyone who does not come from the same social and cultural background as we do. If a person does not belong to our tribe, we're unwilling to connect with them.

Hakhnasat orḥim means being willing to open ourselves up to other worlds, and to bring them into our home, our fortress. A couple interested in adding a child to their world also brings a third partner into the house – one who will frequently disturb them night and day, who may delay their professional advancement, and add no small measure of worry to their lives. Abraham and Sarah's last test before bringing a child into this world was their endless willingness to include everyone who came within their purview. This is why the Torah connects these two stories.

Israeli society is constantly in an uproar, which tends to sharpen the positions of the different groups within it, and this is a good thing. But at the same time, we must learn to bring guests into our home, to include other perspectives, so that we might enable the birth of new possibilities.

Ḥayei Sara

Ironically, the *parasha* called "*Ḥayei Sara*," literally, "Sarah's life," does not speak of her life, but rather of her death and burial. Sarah dies at the age of 127, relatively young for those times (Abraham lives to be 175, and Isaac to 180). According to the Sages' understanding, Sarah's death was related to her mistaken understanding that Isaac was slaughtered on Mount Moria in the *Akeda* story that is told in the last *parasha*. Abraham now seeks to bury Sarah, and to do that he needs a burial cave. Because he is new to the land, and people generally would bury their family members in the family plot, it is no surprise that he has a hard time finding a burial place. The Torah dedicates a long section to the description of the purchase of Maarat HaMakhpela. A story that could have been summarized in a verse or two is turned into a detailed description, twenty verses long, of tortuous bargaining with Ephron, the owner of the cave. The negotiation ends with the payment of an astronomical price – four hundred silver shekels, in return for a piece of land with very little real estate value – a terrible deal. Why does the Torah insist on telling us all this?

Traditional commentaries suggest two opposite approaches to understand the depth of this story. Rabbi Abraham ibn Ezra suggests that the detailed description comes to show Abraham how God will keep His promises to him. The land was promised, and here you are beginning to actualize that prophecy.

The Midrash sees things from the opposite perspective, telling the following story: Moses was sent to Pharaoh with the demand to free the Jewish people from their slavery. Pharaoh sends Moses and Aaron away, defeated, and even increases the people's workload, making them collect their own straw and hay in order to produce bricks, while maintaining the same daily quota they had until then. Obviously, they are unable to meet this demand, and suffer beatings from the Egyptian taskmasters. From within this desperate circumstance, Moses turns to God and says: "Why, Lord, have you brought harm to this people? Is this why You sent me?" (Exodus 5:22). I went to speak to Pharaoh, Moses says, but I failed to have them freed, and their lot was made even more difficult! According to the Midrash, God answers Moses with the following words: "Woe for those who are lost and not found" (Sanhedrin 111a), meaning: "Woe for the great figures of the past who are no longer with us. You, Moses, are upset by Pharaoh's refusal, while I remember Abraham to whom I promised the entire land, and when his wife died, he did not even have a piece of land in which he could bury her, but nevertheless, he did not complain." As opposed to Ibn Ezra, who understood the story of buying the cave as a testimony to the fulfillment of God's promise, the Midrash sees it as an expression of its lack of fulfillment, and of Abraham's greatness for not complaining about it.

These two approaches would seem to reflect two different ideological perspectives regarding the building of the land and the nation, in those times as well as in our own. There are those who think that the divine promise regarding the inheritance of the land exempts them from the need for any human, natural initiative, for if God promised, He will certainly fulfill His promise, even if we do nothing. In contrast to this position, Ibn Ezra suggests that God fulfills His promise through our own human initiative. Let's see how God's promises are fulfilled: through tremendous exertion and effort on Abraham's part. In the difficult moments after his beloved's passing, Abraham understood that he must move forward to the next stage of inheriting the land. From the concrete need to acquire a burial plot arose the need to acquire an inheritance in the Land of Israel. "A dunam here, a dunam there, one mound after another." God's promise stands, but human action is our own responsibility.

The Midrash, on the other hand, expresses what many feel in their heart, that God will do everything from above. Throughout the two-thousand-year exile, prior to the Zionist movement, many Jews espoused this position. But even according to the Midrash, Abraham does not miss the opportunity. Perhaps he thought initially that God should offer him the land on a silver platter, but when he understood that God does not work in this way, he did not sit idly by. Abraham did not question God, nor did he complain; he understood that "even if the labor is not his to finish, he cannot completely exempt himself from it."

It seems that the eternal tension between the vision and the ability to achieve it is at the very heart of the story of the purchase of Maarat HaMakhpela; and not only there, but also at the very heart of the Jewish people's history.

Toledot

Parashat Toledot offers an expansive picture of the troubled relationship of the twins, Esau and Jacob. However, in between the storms that rage within Isaac's family, the Torah inserts a very strange story with a contemporary air. Our forefathers had great herds of plentiful sheep and cattle, and to keep them hydrated, they needed significant amounts of water. As Israel is not overly blessed with springs and rivers, Abraham needed to dig multiple wells. Scripture describes what follows: "And the Philistines envied him. Now all the wells which his father's servants had dug in the days of Abraham his father, the Philistines had stopped them, and filled them with earth" (26:14–15).

Isaac, the son, returns to re-dig the wells that his father

had dug, and Scripture notes and emphasizes that he calls them by the same names used by his father. At this point, a fight breaks out between Isaac's shepherds and the Philistine shepherds over the water, and the wells are renamed: "Esek" and "Sitna."

The naïve reader may ask why the locals should oppose the digging of wells in a dry, arid region? Isn't it in their interest to develop the water sources so that they and their flock will be able to benefit?

Our Sages also had a hard time understanding the Philistines' behavior, suggesting various alternatives to explain their strange reaction. There are those who explained that the Philistines were concerned that digging wells would help their enemies conquer their territory, or that they thought that digging wells would negatively impact the land quality. Others explain that the Philistines did not want the children of Abraham to have a sense of ownership over the land, and wanted to dissuade them by stopping up their wells.

Scripture seems to suggest yet another solution: jealousy. A person who sees his neighbor being industrious, and succeeding to extract the very best from the land, may feel a sense of jealousy which can lead to one of two reactions. The first is that "the envy of sages causes wisdom to multiply" – he might want to learn from his friend's success and try to replicate it. The second possibility is envy that expresses itself mostly in the desire to destroy his fellow's achievements, a feeling of "neither you nor I will have it."

There is nothing new under the sun. In almost every place it was active, the Zionist movement to settle the land brought great blessings to the land's residents, both Jewish and non-Jewish. A land that was desolate and full of swamps, a land plagued by disease, was transformed by the Jewish settlers into a blooming oasis. What was the reaction of the Arab residents of the land at the time? Was it acceptance, and a desire to learn from the pioneers' successes, or jealousy that led to hatred and destruction?

Isaac did not lose hope, even after renaming the second well "Sitna," because the Philistines had fought with him over it as well. He moved and dug a new well, called "Reḥovot": "Now the Lord has given us space, and we will flourish in the land" (26:22).

Ultimately, the land will belong to those who love it and invest all of their energies in building and maintaining it. Those who seek to banish others with hatred, by stopping up wells or with explosives, will only find themselves lost in an endless sea of hate.

Vayetzeh

Parashat Vayetzeh is one of the longest *parashot* in the Torah: 148 verses. It deals primarily with Jacob's escape from Esau to the house of his uncle, Laban the Aramean. There, in the years of his exile, Jacob is blessed with children, twelve sons and one daughter (according to our Sages' tradition, another twin daughter, who is not mentioned in Scripture, was born alongside each son). Jacob also amassed great wealth during his time in exile, and at the end of the *parasha*, he returns to Israel. When he had left, Jacob was accompanied by angels whom he saw in his dream, ascending and descending a ladder; upon his return, he also meets angels, and he names the location where he enters the land after them, calling it "Maḥanayim."

For this *parasha,* I want to focus our gaze on a visual characteristic that seems to be connected to the physical appearance of the story, and not to its content. Every book or story has paragraphs, creating spaces between different topics. In Scripture, there are paragraphs that are called "*parshiyot.*" These come in two types: open and closed *parshiyot*. As opposed to the division into weekly portions, which is relatively late (created in Babylonia over 1,500 years ago to enable the entire Torah to be read in the synagogue over the course of a year), the division into closed and open *parshiyot* is very ancient.

The closed *parasha* is delineated by a space nine letters long, while the open *parasha* is marked by the following section beginning on an entirely new line. In general, after a number of verses, we will encounter either a closed or an open *parasha*. In the *Ḥumash,* as opposed to in the Torah scroll, they will mark an open *parasha* with the letter *peh* (*petuha*) and a closed one with the letter *samekh* (*setuma*), in order to save space.

Surprisingly, in the unusually long *parasha* of *Vayetzeh,* there is not a single open or closed *parasha*. This is puzzling. Wouldn't it have been proper to break up the different parts of the story here and there? What is so special about this *parasha,* which is intentionally written without any divisions?

The Sages suggest that the purpose of these breaks in the text is to allow us, the readers, to reflect and process between one paragraph and the next, in order to deepen our understanding of what we just read.

It would seem that, as far as *Parashat Vayetzeh* is concerned, the Giver of the Torah wanted to teach us that sometimes, there is no need to understand a story that is still in process and sometimes it is even impossible to do so. To gain a partial understanding can be a waste of time, because the story can only truly be understood at its end.

Parashat Vayetzeh is the story of Israel's exile. Jacob flees from his brother who seeks to kill him. But in exile, his troubles do not cease. Laban, who initially flattered him, tries to deceive him in every possible way, and later tries to rob him of his possessions, and to wage war against him. "The actions of the fathers are a sign for the sons": This *parasha* represents all of Jewish suffering throughout history. But it is precisely in this place of exile that Jacob founds a great family that his predecessors did not merit in the Land of Israel. Do we understand why? No. Many have tried to provide rationales and explanations for the Jewish fate in exile, but whatever we may explain will only be a partial answer.

This is what this *parasha* teaches us with its crowded lines lacking any spaces between them, as if to tell us: Don't even try to understand until we reach the end. To understand the secret of our existence as a nation, we need to read the entire story from beginning to end. Only then can we understand our destiny, and the meaning of each chapter in our history. As the verse states: "Then will our mouths fill with laughter" (Psalms 126:2). Only in the future will we understand the meaning of all the pain that we have experienced. The promise with which Jacob sets out on his journey, God's promise to bring him back to Israel, is waiting to be fulfilled. Until then, it is forbidden to take any breaks.

We don't need to waste too many words translating this idea into our contemporary reality. The difficulties and dangers we experience cause many people to ask: "Why? How long will we experience this?" *Parashat Vayetzeh* teaches us not to stop, not to take a break between one *parasha* and the next in order to rest. May it be God's will that His promise to Jacob be fulfilled: "I am with you. I will protect you where you go…until I have done what I have spoken of to you" (28:15).

Vayishlaḥ

The beginning of *Parashat Vayishlaḥ* tells the story of Jacob's complicated return to Israel after his twenty-year exile. Jacob sends messengers (perhaps these were human messengers, and some say that they were angels) to investigate Esau's intentions. They return from their mission and report that it would seem that Esau intends to go to war, and to prove this, they note that he is marching at the head of a troop four hundred men strong. Jacob is exceedingly concerned, and he reacts with three concrete steps. He prays, sends a large gift with hundreds of animals, and prepares himself for battle. In the end, it turns out that it was (perhaps) all a false alarm. Esau decided to turn over a new leaf in his relationship with Jacob, and was looking for ways to live peacefully with him.

Jacob then enters the land and comes to the area of

Shekhem. Jacob's daughter, Dinah, goes for a stroll in the area, and is raped by the son of the local chieftain. Simeon and Levi, Jacob's sons, cleverly organize a revenge attack and free their sister. Jacob sharply rebukes his sons for their actions. He does this somewhat in our *parasha,* but more at the end of his life, in *Parashat Vayeḥi,* when he will say: "Simeon and Levi are brothers; weapons of violence their wares. Let me never join their council, nor my honor be of their assembly" (49:5–6). Toward the end of the *parasha,* Reuben, the firstborn son, also acts improperly with Rachel's concubine, Bilhah, and then we encounter the following verse: "And Israel heard, and the children of Jacob were twelve" (35:22). A puzzling, strange verse. Are we incapable of counting Jacob's children? But this may just be one of the most important verses in the entire history of the Jewish people.

We're used to thinking that our forefathers had some sons who were better and some who were worse. Abraham had Isaac and Ishmael; Isaac had Jacob and Esau. The rest is history. One son was rejected, and the family continued by way of the second son. Scripture does not go into detail regarding the failures of Ishmael and Esau, but it is apparent that they were not deemed worthy to be the moral heirs of Abraham and Isaac, the fathers of the nation.

Jacob has twelve sons. He condemns two of them for

murder that he deemed unjustified; the firstborn, Reuben, was also accused of improper behavior. But despite this, none of them are rejected. They all remain a part of the family. "The children of Jacob were twelve." The verse may even be sharpening this message when it says, "And Israel heard," that is to say, we are no longer talking about the individual, Jacob, but about Israel, father of the Jewish nation. In this role, he will no longer reject anyone whose actions he finds unfavorable.

It seems that from the moment the decision was made that we will function as a nation, we need to learn how to make room for people whom we would not invite over for coffee and cake, and even people with whom we'd prefer not to be neighbors. The Torah emphasizes this when it says that, even when they have sinned, Jacob's children are still his children, an inseparable part of the nation.

It's difficult to overestimate the importance of the lesson that this *parasha* teaches us. If we would only understand that we will always be the full count of Jacob's children; if we would only internalize that we will never all be cut from the same cloth, and that this is our pride. If we would only accept that, despite our differences, we can belong to one nation and one state – then even the sharpest, most polarizing discourse would allow us to create a diverse society whose members can live in peace with one another. Only then will we merit to fulfill the verse: "And the children of Jacob were twelve."

Vayeshev

When reading the story of Joseph and his brothers, one can't help but cringe. We've already become accustomed to the tensions between Ishmael and Isaac, and between Jacob and Esau, but in these cases we were able to find comfort in the fact that, in the end, they were conflicts between different nations (even if they share a parent or two). When we're talking about Jacob's sons, however, about the foundations of the Jewish people, it's hard to find comfort. How can adult brothers get to a point of such deep hatred that they plot to kill or to sell off their younger orphan brother? How can it be that jealousy and hatred push them so far? We can assume that they understand the severity of their actions, because they try to hide them from their father in different ways.

The verses describe a troubled relationship that begins with Joseph speaking ill of his brothers to their father. We would call him a tattletale, or perhaps a stooge. The verses don't reveal to us the content of Joseph's words, or whether they were truthful or fabricated. Some of the Sages claim that Joseph accused Leah's sons of treating the concubines' sons improperly, or of other immoral behaviors. The fact that the Torah skips over the details of the talebearing attests to the fact that that is not really what matters here. A seed of hatred begins to send forth tendrils and to grow in the family. The tension increases when the brothers see how their father prefers Joseph over them. Jacob even makes special clothing, the *ketonet passim* (37:3), for him, which appears to be some kind of royal garment, or perhaps something akin to designer clothing in our time. What brother would not be jealous when he sees his father discriminating against him? The Torah does not spare words in describing the mounting tension in the family. Joseph begins to dream of sheaves in the field that bow down to his sheaf, and despite his brothers' sharp response, saying, "Do you mean to rule over us?" (37:8), he continues and tells them of a second dream, in which he sees the sun, moon, and eleven stars bowing down to him. What happens next is entirely predictable. At the first opportunity they have, the brothers try to kill him, to be rid of him and his dreams once and for all.

The average reader wonders about the logic of the storyline: Why did Joseph choose to tell his brothers stories that would surely enrage them even more? Didn't he understand the trouble he was getting himself into? Wouldn't it have been better to just let these dreams come true on their own, and for their veracity to be demonstrated without the need for words, or alternatively, to just let them fade away, if they were false? Wasn't Joseph aware of the impact of his words on his relationship with his brothers and their attitude toward him?

The key phrase to focus on, it seems, is "They could not say a peaceful word to him" (37:4). While some of the Sages see this as a kind of praise of the brothers, that they would not speak deceitfully, these words still contain a terrible criticism. The estrangement between Joseph and his brothers was so great that they couldn't even exchange pleasantries with him: "Good morning," "How are you?" If the brothers had been able to speak with Joseph, perhaps they would have been able to justify those actions that he thought he needed to relate to his father. Had they spoken to Jacob, perhaps he could have explained to them why he had decided to spoil Joseph with a special garment. But when the brothers are unable to speak – that is when the troubles begin. Joseph, who shares his dreams, doesn't have any idea of what is going on around him, and he doesn't understand how severe and dangerous his situation is. That is why he allows himself to tell of dreams that upset the entire family (including his father), and that is why he does not hesitate to go by himself to his brothers in Shekhem. He doesn't understand that they have a problem with him. All this is the result of the failure to communicate that begins with "And they could not speak a peaceful word to him."

The Hasmonean kingdom, which flourished for around two hundred years, failed on account of the very same issue. One of the main reasons for its downfall was the refusal of different parts of the community to engage in a discourse regarding the proper way to fight Rome, and the relationship between the priesthood, the sages, and royalty. This situation is very familiar to us in our daily lives: in our relationships, in our family, and at work. The solution is to talk to each other, and to speak peacefully.

Miketz

The main storyline of *Parashat Miketz* is the story of Joseph's rise from prison, where he is cast because of the accusations of Potiphar's wife. Later in the *parasha,* Joseph's charade with his brothers is related in great detail.

Two of Pharaoh's ministers, the chief cupbearer and the chief baker, are imprisoned along with Joseph. They both have dreams, and Joseph does an excellent job interpreting them. Thereafter, Pharaoh also dreams two dreams that trouble him: one about skinny cows swallowing fat cows, and the second about empty sheaves swallowing full ones. In both cases, the weak and lacking consume the strong, without showing any sign of having done so. The cupbearer remembers that in jail, he met a Hebrew who knew how to interpret dreams, and he recommends that Pharaoh use his services. Indeed, Joseph interprets them successfully, and even suggests practical ways to cope with the years of famine that the dreams predict. Pharaoh is impressed by Joseph's talents and creativity, and appoints him to be his viceroy. Part of the dream spoke of a famine that would come upon the land; and indeed, the entire Middle East suffers from a difficult famine, forcing Joseph's brothers to descend to Egypt from their home in Israel in order to buy food. Joseph discovers them and accuses them of spying. After an interrogation, he allows them to return home, but only after they promise to commit that they will bring their younger brother Benjamin back to Joseph. Jacob is reluctant to send the brothers back because he fears for what may happen to Benjamin. He finally agrees only after the entreaties and promises made by Judah. On their second visit to Egypt, Joseph instructs his servants to plant his silver cup in Benjamin's pack, and then blames him for stealing it.

The main question that occupied the commentaries regarding this *parasha* is the attempt to understand Joseph's actions toward his brothers, and especially toward his father, Jacob. Joseph had not seen his father for over twenty years, and did not try to reach out and connect with him all that time. It doesn't take very much imagination to understand the agony of an aging father who lost his favorite son who was killed. Isn't Joseph aware of this? Why isn't he sensitive to his father's pain? Why doesn't Joseph make an effort to let Jacob know where he is?

There are many attempts made to understand Joseph's thinking. Scripture holds no clear clues to explain his actions. We will follow one particular commentary, from which we can also learn much for our own time.

Joseph is very angry about what his brothers did to him. He has not forgotten their attempt to kill him, which was then turned into the sale to the band of Ishmaelites. He wonders whether there is any possibility of sustaining a family when a brother plots to kill or banish his brother, whatever the reason may be.

There is only one way for him to answer this question – by testing his brothers' behavior toward Benjamin, the other brother from his mother's house. He seeks to test whether they feel a sense of solidarity toward him, and whether or not they are willing to sacrifice on his behalf. True, the brothers sinned and wronged him in a way that is difficult to forgive, but mistakes can happen. The important questions to ask are: Did they learn something from this mistake, and are they trying to fix it? The brothers' test will be: What will they do when their brother Benjamin is accused of theft and put into jail? Will they come to his rescue, or abandon him in his time of need? Joseph is ready to cause his father twenty years of pain in order to allow a reuniting that will be more than skin deep. He wants to test how far the sons of Leah are willing to go for the son of Rachel, their mother's rival. Have they learned the lesson from the sale of Joseph; there is a red line in brotherly relationships that must not be crossed even toward a brother who doesn't follow their path? Brothers don't sell their brother to non-Jews, and they are certainly not meant to injure him themselves. Joseph, who wants to bring about a renewed unification of the family, wants to be sure that it will be a true, deep connection.

Many times throughout our history, we have had to stand up against enemies from the outside. Some of those times, we did not have an internal consensus about how to manage the conflict. The lesson that Joseph is teaching his brothers, and us as well, is that even if we don't agree, even when we argue, we remain brothers. We need to bear the responsibility for each other's mistakes, and we must never, ever abandon a brother.

Vayigash

Parashat Vayigash begins where we left off the previous *parasha*: The Egyptians are demanding Benjamin's head, because he is accused of stealing the royal goblet. But the brothers, led by Judah, do not give in easily, and try to negotiate his release. The *parasha* begins with a pained monologue that Judah delivers to the Egyptian monarch, that is, Joseph. Judah describes in heartrending words how the monarch has been unreasonably targeting the brothers. He continues with a description of Jacob's personal family tragedy, the elderly father who lost first his beloved wife, and then their son, and explains what will likely happen if Benjamin stays in Egypt. The drama reaches a climax when we are told that Joseph cannot hold back any longer, and asks that all the Egyptians leave the room. And then – "And he wept aloud.... And Joseph said unto his brethren: 'I am Joseph; is my father still alive?' His brothers were so bewildered at his presence that they could not answer him" (45:2–3). If the verse is read slowly and appropriately, it is easy to imagine the incredible tension that is broken in that awesome moment. Joseph, who just a moment ago acted as a cruel, unfeeling ruler, transforms suddenly into the younger brother who bursts into tears, and all he can say is: "I am Joseph; is my father still alive?"

The question itself is strange because Judah had just told him that his elderly father still lives. They obviously couldn't have known if Jacob had died after they had set out on their journey. But I want to focus specifically on the brothers' reaction to Joseph's surprising revelation. Scripture says that they couldn't say a word to him. They were in shock from this unexpected turn of events. The Sages understood this shock in a completely different way. The Midrash in Genesis Rabba (93:10) describes what was happening in that scene with these words: "Woe to us from the day of judgment, woe to us from the day of rebuke!" In other words, if the brothers could not withstand Joseph's rebuke, how will we withstand God's rebuke? This seems to be a strange comparison, as Joseph did not make any claims against them, nor did he accuse them of anything. All he said was, "I am Joseph. How is father doing?" Where did the Sages hear a hint of rebuke or moralizing in Joseph's words?

It could be that the Sages were trying to teach us a fundamental principle relating to human psychology. Most people direct their lives based on their opinions and beliefs. Many of us have unequivocal thoughts and well-formed ideas about many topics, both national and personal. Many people have set ideas about friends, neighbors, political opponents, and others. We often like to give our opponents tags that help us fit ourselves and others into black-and-white categories.

What happens when the way we tag each other blows up in our faces? How will we react if the neighbor we loved to hate, claiming that he is an arrogant uncaring person, is revealed to actually be a loyal and genuine friend in a moment of truth? What will we feel if a person we imagined to be a monster suddenly encounters us and we need to change our opinion about him? The Sages call this situation "the day of judgment" and "the day of rebuke." "The day of judgment" here is the day that a person reveals that the truths that they chose to rely on to determine whom to love and whom to hate were fundamentally false. The "rebuke" is the reality that slaps us in the face and puts our thoughts and preconceptions to the test of real life. This is exactly what happens to Joseph's brothers. This was Joseph's great rebuke to his brothers.

What didn't Joseph's brothers think about him? What didn't they say about him? What didn't they attribute to him? After all, they could not speak peacefully with him. But then, in the moment of truth, Joseph says to them: "I am he. That demon that you had built is standing before you. How is our father doing? Is he alive?" Can such a man, whose only concern is the well-being of his father, possibly be a danger to the brothers' peace and prosperity?

The brothers can't respond. Who can respond when the truth is thrown in their face? How many times have we built up preconceptions, and created real or imagined enemies? Then, when we meet them or speak to them, it becomes clear that we had created an imagined world. This is the real rebuke that will cause us pain. This is "the day of rebuke." The day that we understand that we have constructed imagined theories about ourselves and about others. We are all like Joseph's brothers, and we are all like Joseph revealing himself to his brothers and asking: "Is my father still alive?"

Vayeḥi

Parashat Vayeḥi, the final *parasha* in the book of Genesis, describes Jacob's actions in his final days in Egypt. There are two *parashot* in the Torah named for life that speak about death: *Parashat Ḥayei Sara* tells of Sarah's burial and *Parashat Vayeḥi* details Jacob's death. We can understand that the story of the death of these figures says something about the fundamental building blocks of their lives, and of our own.

Jacob's departure from this world begins with an oath that he has Joseph take, to bury him in Israel – an act that is intended to remind his sons where they are meant to return after their exile in Egypt. He then bids farewell to Joseph and his sons, and gives them his blessings. Finally, he takes leave of the rest of his sons, the twelve tribes of Israel, and gives them blessings especially related to what will happen to them in the future. The process reaches its climax with Jacob leaving this world. Scripture continues with a detailed description of his funeral. As he was the father of the viceroy of Egypt, the most important empire of the time, this was an event that made a significant impression on the world.

Jacob's blessings left us with a timeless heritage in the form of his blessing to his grandchildren, Ephraim and Manasseh. Many parents bless their children with this very formula every Friday night: "May God make you as Ephraim and Manasseh." The custom to bless the children in this way did not occur by accident. Jacob explicitly tells Joseph: "Israel will bless with you, saying, 'Let God make you like Ephraim and Manasseh'" (48:20). In other words, Jacob predicted that the Jewish people would bless their children in this way, with a blessing that wishes them children as good as Ephraim and Manasseh. Why did Ephraim and Manasseh enjoy this unique merit, rather than Judah, Benjamin, or any of the other brothers? Why are they the brothers who were inscribed on the hearts of the Jewish people as the sons so blessed that all want to be like them?

Is it because, according to tradition, they were the

ones to care for their elderly grandfather when he lived in Egypt, excelling in acts of kindness toward the elderly? Was it because of the many languages that they knew?

It could be that Ephraim and Manasseh actually represent something completely different.

Let's remind ourselves of the context. Joseph descends to Egypt against his will, because he is sold by the brothers. He marries Asenath, daughter of Potiphera, a senior member of the Egyptian government, and they have two children, Ephraim and Manasseh. These children grew up in Egypt, far from the support of a broader Jewish family. Their grandfather and almost all of their family live in Israel. How will they be educated? Will they be able to maintain their Jewish identity in an idolatrous world with a glorious culture? Will they be able to be a part of Jewish tradition?

Jacob meets his grandchildren and discovers, to his great surprise, that although they grew up in a foreign land, they want a connection with him, and to be part of his heritage. According to our Sages' tradition, they even spoke to Jacob in his language, to tell him that even though they grew up in Egypt, and were acquainted with the cultural world that surrounded them, they wanted to be part of the Jewish people, and to use the Hebrew language, a symbol of the traditions of the forefathers.

Jacob, who understands that in the future the Jewish people will be spread among the nations, exposed in every country to the reigning culture, wanted to bless us to be like Ephraim and Manasseh. Then, even when we are surrounded by religions and cultures that are exceedingly far from our Torah, we would know to maintain our uniqueness and our identity. Therefore, he sets Ephraim and Manasseh as our model, so that we always remember the importance of our connection to the values and traditions of the Jewish people.

POCKET

Exodus

שמות

Shemot

The name of the *parasha,* which is also the name of the book as a whole, is "*Shemot*" – "names" – on account of the opening verses that recount the names of Jacob's children who descended to Egypt because of the famine in Israel. In the very next verse, we read that Jacob and his sons have already died. A new king has arisen over Egypt, one who "did not know Joseph," that is, who forgot everything, or at least pretended to. Thus begins the first exile in Jewish history. The Egyptians subjugate their Jewish guests, requiring them to pay heavy taxes and to perform difficult labor in impossible conditions. This is the background for the events of our *parasha*.

The unique name of the *parasha* and the book highlights a new phenomenon that we did not see in Genesis – most of the heroes in the *parasha* don't have a name, even when we would expect them to. For example, when the Torah recounts the marriage of Moses's parents, it says: "A man of the house of Levi went and married a daughter of Levi" (2:1). They have names, Amram and Jochebed, that the Torah itself will tell us in another five chapters. Why, then, does the Torah hide their names now? The *parasha* also tells us of an "Egyptian man" who hits a "Hebrew man" – both are mentioned without names or any other description beyond their national identity. Subsequently, the Torah records another event, in which two Hebrew men are fighting. When Moses intervenes, he says to the aggressor, "Why are you striking your own neighbor?" (2:13). He receives a sharp response: "Do you intend to kill me as you killed the Egyptian?" (2:14). Here too, we do not hear the names of the combatants (the Sages claim that this is Dathan and Abiram, but the text itself does not reveal this).

What is the meaning of this silence?

It would seem that Scripture wants to immerse us in a world in which people are subjugated, oppressed, and nameless. Perhaps numbers are engraved on their arms, or perhaps they have other identifying marks, but they do not have their personal name. Along with this, our *parasha* also contains the story of the midwives, Shiphrah and Puah, who endanger their lives to deliver Jewish babies in direct contradiction of Pharaoh's order to kill them.

When does the Torah decide to mention the names of its heroes and when does it hide them?

We can suggest the following idea. After the tense altercation between Moses and the two fighting Hebrews, Moses reacts with the words "Surely, the thing has become known" (2:14). On a simple level, it seems that Moses understands that his killing of the Egyptian was discovered, and therefore, he must escape Egypt before the Egyptian authorities find out. But Rashi, following the Midrash, explains Moses's words differently. "The matter that I was wondering about became known to me: What was Israel's sin among the seventy nations that they should be cruelly subjugated? But now I see that they deserve it." In modern parlance, the Midrash is describing Moses's struggle with the question: "What did we do to deserve this?" His conclusion is that we indeed deserve it. If two Jews can beat each other up, and then threaten to hand the one who tries to separate them over to the Egyptian authorities, then it seems as if we have brought these troubles upon ourselves.

Let us return to the matter we mentioned initially. When the Torah describes an event and doesn't mention the names of the individuals involved, it is hinting that these are standard events that are not exceptional; two people hitting each other and telling on one another isn't news. Someone from the house of Levi marrying a Levite woman isn't news; marriages happen all the time. But two heroic women who dare to deliver Jewish babies under the nose of the Egyptian despot, exposing themselves to grave danger – these are true heroes, a rarity in the oppressive Egyptian milieu.

The transition from the book of Genesis to the book of Exodus is the transition from individuals and families to a nation. On this path, there will occasionally be individuals who stand out as exceptions to the norm. The description of social behavior will not be marked by noting names; this is everyone's behavior. We are all a part of it, and therefore it is part of our identity as individuals and as a society, and we must respond to it as such.

Va'era

Parashat Va'era's story is a direct continuation of what was described in the preceding chapters. God sends Moses to speak to Pharaoh and tell him to release the Jewish people from Egypt. Pharaoh, for his part, refuses, even increasing the workload of the Hebrew slaves, so that the people would "not regard lying words" (5:9). Pharaoh thinks that they have too much free time, and therefore they spend their time with vain thoughts of possible redemption from their servitude. He gives the order to make their conditions more difficult: from now on, he will not be satisfied merely with difficult construction work; rather, he orders them to collect the raw materials to make the bricks as well.

Moses expresses his frustration at the failure of his

first national mission as a leader with the words "Why have You brought harm to this people?" (5:22).

Our *parasha* begins with God's answer to Moses, in which He promises him that, despite it all, Israel's redemption is imminent, and that God will take them out of Egypt and bring them to the Promised Land. Moses conveys the message to the people, but they refuse to listen, "in the brokenness of their spirit, and the brutal labor" (6:9). Indeed, who has the patience to hear future predictions about freedom and equality while struggling just to stay alive under the heavy Egyptian bondage.

Scripture continues with God's command to Moses to return to Pharaoh and to demand that he release the Jewish people. But this time, Moses stubbornly argues: "The Israelites, You see, have not listened to me. How then will Pharaoh listen?" (6:12). If the Jews don't listen to me (perhaps because of my speech impediment), how will Pharaoh? The verses don't record God's response to Moses, but continue laconically: "The Lord spoke to Moses and Aaron; and He charged them with regard to the Israelites, and to Pharaoh, king of Egypt, to bring the Israelites out of the land of Egypt" (6:13). It is as if there is a dialogue of the deaf; Moses says, in simple words, that he has no one with whom he can speak, and God responds: Speak with Israel and Pharaoh.

Our Sages suggest two ways to think about these verses. The first is presented in the Jerusalem Talmud. They saw in this verse a kind of criticism of one of the leading elite classes of the Jewish people of those days. Not all Jews suffered in Egypt; according to the Sages, some of the people even subjugated their fellow Jews in Egypt. With this unfortunate reality as background, God tells Moses that there is no chance that Pharaoh will let the Jewish people out of Egypt if the Jews subjugate and enslave one another. One can't come to Pharaoh with unclean hands and ask him to do what we ourselves are incapable of doing. Therefore, the verse emphasizes that Moses needs to speak to the children of Israel, and only afterward to Pharaoh. We cannot demand from other nations that which we won't demand of ourselves. Perhaps this is also the reason that the Jews did not believe Moses and didn't listen to him. Will he succeed in convincing the upper echelons of Jewish society before making demands of Pharaoh?

By contrast to this interpretation, Rashi, greatest of the Torah commentators, who in his commentaries demonstrates great love for the Jewish people in their time of need, explains the verses in the following way: "He commanded him to them, to lead them with patience and to tolerate them." According to this explanation, God is responding directly to

Moses's claim that no one is willing to listen to him. Perhaps this is the initial impression left on Moses after speaking to them, but Moses's first lesson in leadership of the Jewish people is patience, patience, and more patience. The Jews must be spoken to calmly, and most of all, Moses must learn to tolerate them. The Jews are like the *sabra,* prickly on the outside but sweet on the inside. It takes time to understand this; one needs pleasantness and even more patience. God commands Moses to lead them gently and to tolerate them, even when it is difficult.

Bo

In *Parashat Bo,* the Torah continues to describe the last three plagues, the plague of locusts, of darkness, and the killing of the firstborn. This last plague is sent to the Egyptians on the last night, the night that our forefathers left Egypt.

The night that Israel left Egypt was prepared in meticulous detail. The Jewish people were commanded to take lambs (considered sacred in Egyptian culture), to keep them in their houses for four days (in full view of their Egyptian neighbors), to slaughter them, and to paint their doorposts with their blood. The formal reason for this command was to allow the destroying angel, who was attacking the Egyptians, to distinguish between the Egyptians and the Jews: "And when I see the blood, I will pass over you, and there shall be no plague be upon you" (12:13). But this explanation raises many questions. God is performing powerful miracles, like the plagues of blood and frogs – and yet He needs signs to help Him distinguish between Jews and Egyptians?! The Torah itself had described extensively how the Egyptians had been afflicted in other plagues, like darkness and hail, while the Jews had not suffered from those plagues at all, as it says: "And all the children of Israel had light in their dwellings" (10:23). Can't God know on His own who are His enslaved people, and who are the oppressing Egyptians?

Perhaps the command to slaughter the lambs and spread their blood as a sign on the house was a sign for us, not for God.

A nation of slaves is mired in its enslavement and day-to-day worries. Many don't have any faith in their ability to escape the cycle of suffering and oppression. Others ask themselves: Maybe this is just another messianic delusion that will end in disaster? Other groups are worried about how the Egyptians will react to seeing their slaves, in a sudden display of national and religious independence, slaughtering their gods in plain view. All of these fears and concerns are very understandable. But after God had served everything up to the nation on a silver platter, bringing nine plagues that profoundly damaged the Egyptians and their economy, it is as if now He is saying to the nation: "I have done My part, now you need to do your part." A person cannot be redeemed against his will. He can be given financial help. He can and should be given tools, personal security, and the like. But it is impossible to decide on his behalf to become a free person. That is a decision he must make for himself. The command to paint the doorposts with blood is akin to a request of a person to decide where he belongs, and to whom he is connected. It isn't much, but it is the minimum required to leave the cycle of subjugation.

No wonder, then, that the mezuza became one of the identifying marks of the Jewish people throughout the generations. It isn't a more or a less important mitzva than any other, but it is a mitzva that comes to define the identity of the home. There is a compound inner meaning to the act of painting the doorpost. A person must do something for himself, by himself, and cannot solely rely on someone else, even if it is God. In addition, the beginning of the redemption of the nation is the expression of the desire to identify with the nation. Someone who understands that they have a part to play in their own redemption, and that they must give public expression to their attachment to their nation, is one who can be redeemed.

Beshallaḥ

The Exodus from Egypt was characterized by some of the most remarkable miracles of the Scriptural period; beginning with the plague of blood, which filled the famous Nile with blood, and ending with the plague of the firstborn, which afflicted every family, leaving no house in which cries were not heard. Between these two plagues, the Egyptians suffered from a whole range of calamities, that we would only wish upon our very worst enemies.

And yet, we find the very God, who performed all of these miracles and took the Jewish people out of Egypt, facing a difficult dilemma. The first stage of the mission was a success. Pharaoh gives in and frees the nation. However, there is a problem with the second stage and the journey to the Land of Israel. After two hundred years of exile, the Jewish people is not accustomed to wars. Yet on the way to the Promised Land, they will likely encounter aggressive forces (such as the Philistines, for example) who will initiate battles with them. If that happens, the nation may regret the whole endeavor, and turn tail for Egypt: "Lest the people repent when they see war and return to Egypt" (13:17). As a result, God changes the planned trajectory, and leads the people by way of the desert, toward the Sea of Reeds. There, they encounter a new problem, as Pharaoh recovers, and manages to enlist the last vestiges of Egyptian motivation to chase after the Israelites.

Two questions arise as we read this story. God had performed so many miracles. Couldn't He simply perform one more small miracle to deal with the danger from the Philistines? Couldn't He who will split the sea in another week and created ten plagues in the last year just send boulders from the heavens to end the potential threat from the Philistines or the Canaanites? We cannot help but ask about our own people as well: Are the Jewish people still skeptical about their ability to overpower other nations after seeing all of the miracles and signs, the blood, frogs, lice, etc.? Is a nation of hundreds of thousands overcome by the fear of a few hundred soldiers on horses?

It seems that it's easy to redeem a nation from bondage with a few plagues and miracles, but changing people's mindset is much more difficult. You can take Israel out of Egypt, but it's much harder to take the mindset of Egypt out of Israel. The mindset of Egypt is the fear aroused by the threatening voice of every despot, the lack of confidence in our ability to change the world without worrying about what others will say, the submission to one's habits, and the lack of confidence in one's ability to challenge them. Slave habits that have been ingrained in a nation over the course of hundreds of years cannot simply disappear in an instant. Even God can't change them, so to speak, unless we ourselves are willing to do so.

But it seems that even God did not hurry to do this, nor did He think that miracles and wonders could solve every problem. Apparently, a direct blow is not always the proper or the best solution. At times, from a broad perspective, the correct thing to do might indeed be a long sojourn in the desert, rather than an immediate confrontation. It can be better to save the development of bravery and military capacity for a later time.

Human society constantly yearns for instant solutions, right here and right now. We wish that the nightmare of the Iranian threat would be behind us, but instead we hear only of economic sanctions, or other actions that seem all too slow. We wish we could instantly solve issues like the housing crisis, inequality in the military draft, and many others. But a courageous view of reality reveals that magical, instant solutions exist only in the movies.

Sometimes the direct blow and the sharp confrontation are the correct solution. But human history, and each of our own personal histories, teach us that in most cases, overcoming difficulties is a process that needs to mature and develop. In this way, the solution is one that goes deep to the root of the problem, and therefore, ultimately, is all the more effective.

Yitro

There are few *parashot* that bear the name of an individual. That it is the name of a non-Jew is even more rare. There are three individuals who enjoyed this privilege: Noah, Jethro, Moses's father-in-law, and Balak, king of Moab. Noah, however, is at the very center of an enormously important event – the flood; and the story of Balak, who seeks to stop the nation on their way to the Promised Land, is necessary so that we understand the nation's history in the desert. The mention of Jethro, on the other hand, seems rather unnecessary, and certainly in such a central *parasha* as that which tells the story of the giving of the Torah at Sinai.

Who is Jethro? Moses, fleeing Egypt after killing an Egyptian who beat a Jewish slave, marries the daughter of

Jethro, the priest of Midian. According to our tradition, Jethro was one of the most important priests in the idolatrous cult of Midian; there was almost no form of idol worship that he had not tried. While Moses was trying to free his nation from Egypt, Jethro was with Moses's wife and his two young grandsons. Now that the Jewish people had left Egypt to the Sinai desert, Jethro seeks to reunite the family. The Torah dedicates an entire chapter to tell of Jethro's arrival at the Israelite camp. He is not satisfied with being a momentary guest of his son-in-law and daughter; he starts giving advice and even voicing criticism. He sees that Moses is administering the justice system with excessive centralization and tells him that there is no chance that he will be able to sustain such a system. Moses is convinced and changes his approach; he appoints ministers of the thousands and the hundreds – basic administrative structures to allow for the management of a nation that numbers in the millions.

This is strange. Here we are, on the eve of the giving of the Torah on Mount Sinai, one of the most significant and profound events in Jewish history, and in human history, and the Torah sees fit to dedicate its time to such a seemingly marginal issue! Why did this non-Jew merit that the *parasha* of the giving of the Torah would be named after him? There are Sages who suggest that Jethro actually arrives in the desert many days after the giving of the Torah, which makes it all the more difficult to understand why it is mentioned specifically here.

It would seem that someone is intent on sending us a message, via Jethro, that we need to receive before the giving of the Torah.

In another moment, the Torah will be received from on high, from the Master of the universe. In a moment, we will be told what a tremendous honor it is to belong to a nation that received fundamental values that will be the cause of dramatic changes in world history. "You will be My treasure among all the peoples, although the whole earth is Mine. A kingdom of priests and a holy nation you shall be to Me" (19:5–6). It is highly probable that, as a result, we will experience a sense of tremendous exaltation, and rightfully so.

An important concern which accompanies such an experience is that all this exaltation and the importance of our task will "go to our head." Perhaps we will feel haughty, and won't know how to listen to the other, especially to a non-Jew. The concern is that, in the excitement of these events, we will forget that basic human respect, *derekh eretz,* precedes Torah; that we will think that after receiving the Torah, there is no longer any need to simply be a moral, good person, a *mentsch,* in Yiddish.

To counter this, we need Jethro.

The divine Torah given from heaven is glorious and important. No human being could invent the idea of Shabbat, given to us as a gift. A human being would have a hard time summarizing all of the ethical teachings related to property in the words "Thou shall not covet" (20:14).

But before the grand values, be a *mentsch*. Jethro arrives, with all of the emotional baggage that may exist between him and Moses (we all know that a son-in-law and father-in-law don't always get along), and teaches us: Accept the truth from wherever it comes. Moses could have told his father-in-law to "mind his own business" and let him handle matters in the way he sees fit. But he doesn't do that. He understands that one needs to be willing to learn from every person, even if it your father-in-law, even if it is a non-Jew, and even if we have already received the Torah from God.

The ability to listen to Jethro is a necessary precondition before receiving the Torah from God.

Mishpatim

Parashat Mishpatim examines a broad range of laws that come to regulate the relationship between an individual and society: for example, the punishments that relate to murder, theft, damages, irresponsible guardians, and more. The Torah chose to begin this selection of laws with the rules relating to male and female slaves. Yes, to our great astonishment, there is such a thing as legal slavery regulated by the laws of the Torah. The opening verse says thus: "If you buy a Hebrew slave, he shall serve for six years; but in the seventh he shall go forth free, without paying anything" (21:2). If after six years, the slave wishes to stay with his master, he can do so, after having his ear pierced with an awl.

An initial reading of these verses will have the

modern reader shifting uncomfortably in their seat. Two months after the Exodus from Egypt, where we were enslaved; mere weeks after hearing the lofty words "Send out My people that they may serve Me" (7:16), that negate the permission of any person to subjugate another and oblige them to let the other worship their God – we would have expected our Torah to come out clearly against slavery. We would have expected no less than the message that Abraham Lincoln delivered to the American people: an end to slavery, and every man's right to freedom.

In the Midrash, our Sages also express their discomfort with the institution of slavery. For example, they explain the piercing of the slave's ear in the following way: "Let the ear that heard My voice on Sinai when I said, 'For the children of Israel are my slaves,' and not the slaves of slaves, and went and acquired a master for himself be pierced" (Kiddushin 22b).

But still, the matter is troublesome. If we have such a hard time with slavery, why does the Torah allow it?

The Sages did limit the possibility to be sold into slavery to two circumstances. The first is a case of a thief sold by the court to compensate his victims, and the second is a case of financial difficulties which leave a person with no choice but to sell himself into slavery so that he can put clothes on his back. In this way, they clearly sought to signal an orientation which does not allow for the sale of slaves against their will, as was the norm in the ancient world. The Rambam adds that a person is not allowed to sell himself into slavery in order to buy merchandise or utensils, thus negating the possibility of a slave trade.

It appears that when it is impossible to completely negate an idea that is too deeply embedded in society, it is still possible to soften it to the point of transformation. The Torah understood that not all people can be completely independent, and that most of them would be forced to work for hire on others' behalf. Therefore, it created the concept of the "Hebrew slave," which is essentially a type of employee, in our terms. It could be that many modern-day employees would be happy to receive the working conditions of the slave as defined by the Torah.

What is the nature of the relationship between employer and employee? Can he abuse him, and fail to provide basic working conditions? The halakha establishes that the master is not allowed to say to his slave, "'Dig under the grapevines until I come,' nor 'Dig in this place,' if he doesn't need it" (*Mishneh Torah, Hilkhot Avadim* 1:6), because these are tasks without a clear boundary which denigrate the worker. In general, the Sages established that it is forbidden for the master to demand demeaning tasks of his slave, like bringing his clothes to the bathhouse, or taking off his shoes.

The Sages went so far as to say that one who acquires a slave acquires a master for himself. In other words, employing someone became no small headache.

It is impossible and improper to prevent a person from employing his fellow. On the other hand, it is inhumane and immoral to employ someone without giving them basic rights that ensure fair payment. No less important is to ensure humane and respectful treatment.

It would seem that based on this approach, we have an obligation to raise public awareness of the problem of contract workers who do not enjoy the basic rights of a worker in a civilized society. Not only the most vulnerable deserve protection and proper treatment. We need to protect all workers, both foreign and not, independent contractors and steady employees. Are they given the proper respect? This respect begins by education to say "Please" and "Thank you" and ends with fair wages and working conditions.

The Torah defines the proper treatment of the worker as "For it is good for him with you" (Deuteronomy 15:16). Do our workers feel this way today?

Teruma

An enormous mass of freed slaves travels in the very heart of the desert. They just recently successfully escaped the Egyptian empire, and their pursuers drowned in the sea. The group has no independent source of sustenance, and receives a special food called manna every day. This food cannot be preserved from one day to the next, and therefore, every morning, these people must worry about their next meal.

The group's leader ascends Mount Sinai and receives a list of basic instructions to manage the people. Parts of it are entirely foreign to them – like the prohibition against making an idol, or the obligation to observe the Shabbat. He then ascends a second time in order to receive the entirety of the Torah. The whole group, some with greater enthusiasm and some with less, say, "We will obey and listen" to all of the commandments they receive. In modern parlance, they are saying to Moses: "Go for it, let's see where this takes us, what else can He spring on us…"

And then, out of nowhere, in the middle of the desert, God declares: I want a donation "from all whose heart moves them to give" (25:2). One doesn't need too much imagination to picture what the people's reaction to this may have been. "You want money? This is what we came out of Egypt for?? Why should we give? Where is this money going?"

Indeed, the explanation comes immediately: "They shall make Me a Sanctuary and I will dwell in their midst" (25:8). God also wants housing, not just us.

Everyone understands that a person needs a place to pour out his heart to his creator, that is, a house of prayer, or as we would say, a synagogue. But this isn't what the verse states. Scripture emphasizes God's desire to reside in a home. Does God, who has no body or form, need a physical structure?! Is not all the earth His glory and the place of His residence? What lies behind this strange request for a donation?

In the previous sections, the nation has been commanded with tens of laws and statutes, and now, all of the sudden, they are asked to donate. Why would anyone want to donate to building a sanctuary? What's in it for them? Especially when we are talking about people who have survived the trauma of enslavement. Their suspicion of their surroundings, and their concern for the here and now, will certainly make it difficult for them to donate for an unclear, unknown purpose.

It seems that this is exactly the Torah's intention. The verse was precise in saying, "That I may dwell in their midst," that is, within the people, and not "That I may dwell in it" (in the Sanctuary). God does not need a dwelling place; we have a deep desire to host Him within ourselves. It was very easy for us to receive commandments at Mount Sinai since we were accustomed to life as slaves and receiving orders from our master. It appealed to our slave mentality. But our basic human desire was to do things as a consequence of our own good will, not because we were commanded to do them. We wish to be people who do things for our own soul, our own internal good feelings, not merely out of obligation. Indeed, the Torah wants to teach us to recognize the need and the desire to act for our own soul's sake, not just because we need to make a living, or serve someone else's needs. Therefore, the Torah said, "Of every man whose heart moves them to give." We are meant to get used to the fact that it's good to be generous, that it's good to be a "sucker."

A state cannot be built solely on the generosity of its citizens, and therefore, it will collect taxes and require military service. But a society has no chance of survival without a spirit of generosity that inspires its members. Anyone who was ever involved in any volunteer service, whether it is the national guard, Magen David Adom, or any other volunteer body, knows the feeling of satisfaction that fills their heart after this type of activity. *Parashat Teruma* seeks to fill us with the desire to continue volunteering, to know that thus, we build a Sanctuary of good and of giving within ourselves. "And I will dwell in their midst."

Tetzaveh

Parashat Tetzaveh is the second in the series of *parashot* that discuss the building of the Tabernacle. While the previous *parasha* focused mostly on the physical structure of the house that God commanded His people build Him, this *parasha* focuses on the clothing of the priests who serve in the Tabernacle. The centerpiece of this description is the set of eight garments worn by the high priest when he serves in the Sanctuary. This includes a special azure coat decorated with ringing pomegranates. On his breast, the high priest wore a golden plate with twelve precious stones embroidered into it, upon which the names of the tribes of Israel were engraved. The priest's forehead was adorned with a golden headplate called the "*tzitz*." The priests were forbidden from serving in the Temple without their special garments, and one who did so would be punished severely.

What is the significance of this glorious attire? Would it not have been more appropriate to ask of the priests, and especially of the high priest, to serve in more simple clothing, without gold or precious stones, as the high priest does on the Day of Atonement when he enters the Holy of Holies?

The Torah explains the purpose of the clothing thus: "Make sacred vestments for your brother Aaron, for glory and for splendor" (28:2). In other words, this attire is meant to create a splendid, honorable appearance. The Ramban, in his commentary on this verse, further clarifies the meaning of the splendor and glory with the following words: "That he should be honored and splendid with honorable and splendid clothing...for these are royal garments, similar to what royalty in the time of the Torah would wear.... The turban is known even today to be worn by kings and important ministers." But this still begs the question: Why should the priests dress like kings? After all, they're not kings, they are servants in the Temple service. Why should they wear clothes that are inappropriate to their station?

Some of our Sages suggested that the clothes that a person wears create the feeling within the wearer of the importance of their station and the awareness of the mission they have been given. Obviously, putting a "golden ring in a swine's nose" (Proverbs 11:22) will not turn it into a man, but still, one of the ways for a person to make himself aware of the importance of his actions is through the clothes he wears. For this reason, employment advisors will recommend that a person arrive at a job interview in clothing that is appropriate for the job they seek. A person's external appearance, and the first impression that they make, can decide the fate of the meeting. One's clothing affects oneself as well. I remember when I was young, if I would be sick at home, I would always take off my school clothing and wear pajamas. The first sign that I had decided that I was better was when I would put back on my regular clothing: that was how I gave myself the feeling of a healthy person. We all know what our attitude toward an officer in uniform is, as opposed to the very same person in civilian clothing. The Torah demands maximal gravitas of the priests in their service; this must be reflected in their outward appearance as well. In many places, there is a similar expectation of public servants: they must appear in attire that respects themselves and their clients.

At the same time, there is also a danger in overly focusing on external appearances. Sometimes, for all of our concern over our attire, we can forget our true inner desire. Could it be that sometimes we want to impress someone else, or ourselves, with a particular action, when it really isn't true to who we are? We can succeed in impressing everyone, while forgetting our true self. From our *parasha* we learn of the importance and the significance of clothing that is "for honor and splendor"; from within ourselves, we hear the voice of authenticity that wants to maintain its place as the focus of our life. If we will be wise enough to use the "honor and splendor" in the service of inner authenticity, we may succeed to merit the resting of the Divine Presence within us.

Ki Tissa

At the center of *Parashat Ki Tissa* stands one of the most formative stories in Jewish history: the sin of the Golden Calf. The nation is waiting impatiently for Moses's return from Mount Sinai; Moses tarries, and the people turn to Aaron to demand a replacement. Aaron commands them to remove all their gold (and apparently, there was a large quantity), and forms it into a calf. The nation responds with the cry: "These, Israel, are your gods, who brought you out of Egypt" (32:4). God is angry at His people's speedy betrayal, after all that He had done for them since Egypt until this point, and seeks to destroy them and replace them with a new nation, descended from Moses. Moses pleads with God to forgive them, and God is appeased.

One of the questions that has troubled the commentators throughout the generations is: How could a nation that saw all of the miracles in Egypt and at Mount Sinai possibly think that a calf is what brought them out of Egypt?

The simple answer is that even after many miracles, it is difficult to uproot habits of mind and ingrained cultural assumptions. A person who was raised in the world of Egyptian idol worship cannot change his way of thinking in the blink of an eye. A person accustomed to seeing an idol in every house that represented the goddess of fertility cannot easily replace this with something abstract.

The term "a molten calf," "*egel masekha,*" appears in our *parasha* for the first time in the Torah. The word can be explained in a number of ways. "*Masekha*" might be a kind of metal, so that "*egel masekha*" is a metal calf, or, more precisely, a calf that has undergone a process of smelting, as it was made from numerous pieces of gold that needed to be melted together. But there is another meaning of the word "*masekha,*" related to the word "*masakh,*" whose purpose is generally to cover, *lekhasot*; a *masekha* can thus also be a covering for something hidden underneath it (cf. Isaiah 25:7). This, for example, is why a Purim mask is called a "*masekha.*"

Is there a connection between the *masekha* which is

an idol made by a melting process, and a *masekha* mask that covers a person's face?

Our world is covered in masks, some man-made, some of divine creation. The Sages interpreted the meaning of the word "*olam,*" world, as a derivative of the word "*he'elem,*" hiddenness. In other words, the world is something that God hides within; it is a kind of a mask for God. Ancient idol worshippers thought that the sun, the moon, and the stars were the kings of the world; others believed in the superiority of different forces of nature capable of destroying the world. It is not easy to teach a people that behind all of those coverings, an inner power is hidden which rules the world. It is not only nature that can act as a mask of God; political history can play the same role. In Shushan, the capital of Ahasuerus's empire, the city from which came terrible decrees to destroy the Jewish people, there were masks galore. Who is against whom, and why? Did Ahasuerus know of Haman's plans? Why does the king remember to reward Mordekhai for saving him from an assassination attempt only years after it happened? And there are many other, similar questions. The Megilla comes to reveal, *legalot,* that behind all of the chaos hides the Ruler of creation who is guiding the world to the salvation of His people.

One who looks deeply at world politics will find other events that are covered in similar masks. Before the UN voted on the partition plan, it was not at all clear what the results of the vote would be; many countries were influenced by the pressure of the Arab states. It was particularly unclear how the two great superpowers – the United States and the Soviet Union – would vote, which could determine the entire outcome. After the Second World War, these two powers returned to their old rivalry. There was constant bitter conflict between the two over power and influence, which later became the Cold War. In those years, they would not vote in the same way on anything. Moreover, the Soviet Union had opposed Zionism for years. Nevertheless, the two superpowers both voted in favor, as a result of a combination of internal and external considerations that were influenced by a unique set of circumstances, and thus, the path was paved for the establishment of the State of Israel. On the face of it, this was just another regular vote, but actually it was a mask behind which hid the Master of history. This is the mask of the world, the mask that prevents us from seeing deeply into the world's inner meaning and significance.

On a personal level, we also all wear masks. These are usually transparent, so it is hard to discern them.

The story of the Golden Calf serves as a warning against the worship of masks, whether this is a molten idol, or one that serves to hide the presence of God in the world of concealment. It warns us not to forget the truths hidden beneath the masks.

Vayak'hel

After the sin of the Golden Calf, Moses ascends Mount Sinai to beg God to forgive the people. After a number of weeks, on Yom Kippur, Moses descends the mountain with the new tablets in his hands, replacing the ones that he had broken.

Moses brought another message with him as well: that we are to build a Tabernacle. He gathered the people and told them of the command to build and donate to it out of the goodness of their heart.

Scripture is not stingy with its words when it comes to describing the enthusiasm that expressed itself in a tremendous stream of donations from all types of people. These were so plentiful that the professionals told Moses that "the people are bringing too much" (36:5). At this point, a new command is given – stop donating. The verse states: "So the people were restrained from bringing" (36:6). It could have said that "the people stopped giving," but Scripture wanted to emphasize everyone's powerful desire to give more and more of their property and their skills to the building of the Tabernacle.

It is hard not to be impressed by this spirit of generosity, but the Sages read these verses and refused to be enthused. They remembered what the previous *parasha* said about the sin of the Golden Calf. There, too, (almost) everyone donated, with great enthusiasm. And so, the Sages said: "It's hard to understand the true nature of this nation. When they are asked to donate to the Calf, they give, and when they are asked to donate to the Tabernacle, they do so" (Y. Shekalim 1:1).

Many have tried to understand the true nature of the Jewish people. They are asked to give donations to the Golden Calf – and they do. They are asked to donate to the Tabernacle – and they do so as well. But these donations are complete opposites of one another! It would be like donating to an extreme right-wing cause and an extreme left-wing cause at the very same time. How can we understand this special nation?

There would seem to be one central Jewish characteristic that this story teaches us, and that is the trait of enthusiasm.

There is a remarkable phenomenon of enthusiasm that can be discerned among the Jewish people. This can be seen in the throngs of people at stores of brand names from abroad, or the masses that fill jogging trails. This enthusiasm focuses on one brand today, and moves on to a completely different one tomorrow.

It is not a coincidence that we find Jews as active partners in all of the important revolutionary movements in the world, including in the strangest movements and places. When we get excited about something, there is almost no stopping us.

The Talmud tells the strange story of a Jew who passed an idol whose form of worship was for a person to relieve themselves either in front of, or on the idol. The Jew took advantage of this to use the idol in place of toilet paper, as it were. The idol's priest responded: "No one has ever worshipped our idol in such a good and praiseworthy way as this Jew." When Jews do something, they do it with maximum energy and excitement.

This trait has many advantages, as it can bring a person to places that one cannot reach without an overpowering energy. But it can also be very dangerous. It dissipates as fast as it appears. A person who becomes enthusiastic without too much reflection has no reason not to transfer his enthusiasm to something else, even if that represents the very opposite of his initial enthusiasm. We, and our leaders, should not be overly impressed by the enthusiasm of the masses, for it can disappear or be focused in a different direction in an instant. Leaders need to evaluate their actions not based on the enthusiastic voices heard from their public, but based on the logic that is behind them.

Pekudei

Parashat Pekudei, the last *parasha* of the book of Exodus, summarizes the completion of the enormous undertaking that was the building of the Tabernacle. First, it presents a report of the amounts of gold, silver, and copper that were gathered, as well as the types of fabrics that had been donated. Afterward, the *parasha* describes the preparation of the priestly vestments, sparing no detail. Every few verses, Scripture emphasizes that everything was done in accordance with God's command to Moses. In the end, a verse appears that sums up the verses in this *parasha* and the preceding ones: "Thus all the work on the Tabernacle, the Tent of Meeting, was completed. The Israelites did everything exactly as the Lord had commanded Moses" (39:32).

At this point, the people bring all of the parts of the Tabernacle to Moses – the beams, the sockets, the fabrics, the vessels and everything that goes with them, the priestly vestments, the consecrated oil, the Showbread, and the incense. All these are listed in one long, detailed section. Then the summarizing words appear once again: "According to all that the Lord commanded Moses, so the children of Israel did all the work. And Moses saw all the work, and behold, they had done it, as the Lord had commanded, even so had they done it. And Moses blessed them" (39:42–43). Moses inspects everything that was brought before him and sees that everything was truly made according to instructions, and he blesses them for this. We then arrive at the day everyone was waiting for: the moment of the construction of the Tabernacle. God tells Moses that the designated date is the first of the upcoming month of Nisan of that very year.

Everything would seem to be going perfectly. But the Rabbis sensed something dramatic and filled with tension going on between the lines. Why was there a need to bring the vessels for Moses's inspection? Is he meant to be doing quality control? Doesn't he trust Betzalel, whom God Himself had appointed to the job? And what is the purpose of the blessing that Moses gives the children of Israel? The verse that describes the actual construction of the Tabernacle seems strange. On the one hand, Scripture says, "And it was on the first month... the Tabernacle was set up" (40:17). But on the other hand, at the beginning of the very next verse, it says, "And Moses set up the Tabernacle" (40:18). Was the Tabernacle put up by itself, or was it Moses who did it?

The Midrash fills in the details of the story that Scripture only hints to:

> When the work of the Tabernacle was finished, they sat and waited: When will the Divine Presence rest in it? Everyone was pained that the Divine Presence was not residing in it. What did they do? They went to the wise of heart. They said to them: "Why are you sitting? Set up the Tabernacle yourselves, and the Divine Presence will rest among us." They wanted to set it up, but they didn't know how, and when they tried, it fell down. Immediately, they went to Betzalel and Oholiab. They said to them: "You should come and set up the Tabernacle, because you made it. Perhaps it is proper that you should set it up?" They tried to do so, but were not able. They all began talking and gossiping: "Look what this son of Amram (a derogatory nickname for Moses) did to us. He took our money for this Tabernacle, and had us do all this

> work, and told us that God would descend from on high to reside in goat skins, as the verse says (Exodus 25): 'And I will dwell among them.'" (*Tanḥuma*, Pekudei 11).

The Sages relate that after all of the effort invested in building the Tabernacle, it appeared that it was all for nought: the Divine Presence did not rest on the Tabernacle. It seemed to all have been a deception. What else could explain why nothing was working out the way it was supposed to? One could legitimately ask: Why didn't God agree to rest His presence on the Tabernacle immediately? The Midrash answers: "Why weren't they able to put it up? Because Moses was pained that he did not participate with them in making the Tabernacle. How so? The donations were given by the Jewish people, the work was done by Betzalel and Oholiab and the wise of heart. Since Moses was pained, God hid from them, and they could not put it up" (*Tanḥuma* ibid.). God saw Moses's pain and understood that he wanted to take part in the mitzva and wasn't given the opportunity. He wanted the community to see that Moses also had a part in the building of the Tabernacle and would be the one to actually set it up. God holds back from resting His Divine Presence when there are people who were prevented from taking part in the mitzva. Anyone who wants to take part in the building of the nation's Temple is invited to take part, and so long as someone is missing, the joint effort is not complete. Only once Moses is given a part in the work can God's Divine Presence rest.

POCKET Leviticus

ויקרא

Vayikra

The first portion of the third book of the *Ḥumash*, the book of Leviticus, focuses on the Tabernacle: the laws of the sacrifices and the practices related to the holidays and to life-cycle events performed there (such as birth and death, leprosy and the healing process from it). The book is called "*Torat Kohanim*," the "Instruction of the Priests," because large sections in it discuss laws relating to the priests. Our *parasha* focuses on different types of sacrifices that a person can bring: some of one's own desire – called freewill offerings – and some that a person is obligated to bring because of sins that were committed accidentally or intentionally – called obligatory offerings.

For a number of reasons, modern people have a hard

time connecting to the world of sacrifices. There are those who have difficulty seeing the sacrifice of an animal as a way to achieve atonement: they say that this is too simplistic a way for a person to repair their actions. Others are bothered by the fate of innocent animals that pay with their lives for the sins of human beings. And perhaps there are some who are just uncomfortable when they imagine the slaughterhouse for thousands of animals in the place that the Divine Presence is meant to reside. Some of these concerns were shared by the prophets of Israel, who warned against the danger of imagining that an animal sacrifice could come in place of real repentance and personal improvement.

But one phrase in the *parasha* may shed new light on this topic, and reorient our perspective in a novel way.

When Scripture begins to present the different types of sacrifices, it starts with the freewill offerings that a person brings of their own volition, and reads thus: "When one brings of you a sacrifice to the Lord" (1:2). Something about the syntax is not quite right. Proper Hebrew would read: "When one of you brings a sacrifice," since the word "of you" (*mikem*) relates to the group of people who bring sacrifices. The word, then, seems misplaced.

Because of this discrepancy, our Sages concluded that the sacrifice needs to be brought from one's own property and cannot be from stolen goods. The question that immediately arises is: Who would think of bringing a stolen animal as an offering?! But apparently, in life, anything is possible. One person might think that he can achieve atonement for an act of theft by making a significant contribution to the synagogue, or by bringing an impressive offering to the Temple, and therefore the Torah says: "When one brings of you." The offering must be yours; it cannot come at the cost of another. Any progress a person makes in their service of God must come from themselves, and cannot be achieved at someone else's expense. An old ethical precept states: Usually, people are concerned about their own physical well-being, and other people's spiritual well-being. This norm should be turned on its head, so that people are concerned for their fellow's physical well-being, and for their own spiritual well-being. Therefore, the Torah emphasizes: "When one brings *of you*," from your own, and not from someone else.

But an additional possible meaning of the phrase "to bring of you" might hint at the need to sacrifice something of your own – something of your identity and personality. I cannot come closer to God if I don't approach God from within myself, from my own uniqueness and creativity. I cannot rely on anyone else to do it for me. When our Sages saw the world of sacrifices, they wanted us to imagine a world in which we, figuratively, are sacrificing ourselves to our Maker; a world in which a person is committed to their ideas with full authenticity, as if they themselves are being sacrificed on the altar. In times when cynicism often reigns, it is important to remember that there is a world which exists in which people sacrifice for their ideals. There are those who sacrifice themselves for the army, or to settle the land, or for Torah study, or for scientific research. Our world is built by those people who unequivocally sacrifice themselves for their ideals.

The verse "When one brings of you" can bear another meaning, one that is painful and chilling. Throughout our history, the Jewish people has paid in blood for being who we are. From time to time, we are given painful reminders that being Jewish, even in a progressive, enlightened world, can be a symbol and an idea of a vision that the forces of darkness wish to combat. We will continue to aspire to come closer to ourselves and to our vision, even if along the long way, we may need to sacrifice precious souls.

Tzav

Similar to *Parashat Vayikra*, *Parashat Tzav* discusses the laws of sacrifices. The previous *parasha* focused on categorizing the offerings from the point of view of the person bringing the sacrifice, distinguishing between obligatory and voluntary offerings, and between sacrifices from animals and from plants. *Parashat Tzav,* however, discusses these sacrifices from the point of view of the priests working in the Temple. This *parasha* tells us where each sacrifice is slaughtered, which parts are given to the priests, and which are burned on the altar. The most important distinction for our purposes is between the *ola* sacrifice and the *shelamim* sacrifice. The *ola* is entirely consumed by the altar's flames, so that neither the owner nor the priests have any portion in it. In contrast, the *shelamim* sacrifice is eaten by both the owners and the priests.

Our *parasha* begins: "Order Aaron and his sons: This is the law of the *ola*, the burnt offering" (6:2). Our Sages noted the harsh verb used to begin the laws of the burnt offering: "order." The Torah could have used a softer expression, like "This is the instruction of the burnt offering" (6:2), as it does in similar circumstances. Why the need for such direct, confrontational language? Some of the Sages suggest that the word emphasizes the zealousness and efficiency that are demanded of the priests for all generations. Perhaps now, on the first day of their service, all of the priests are excited to serve in the Temple. Perhaps their brethren who are Israelites, who do not merit to serve in the Temple, may even have felt jealous. But Moses wants to encourage the priests and to instruct them to maintain their current level of motivation for all generations, even in the second and third years of their service, even when they get tired of waking up early to perform the Temple rituals. Perhaps the need to encourage the priests also anticipates the generations in which Temple service will demand self-sacrifice in the face of an oppressive Greek government or a cruel Roman governor. In general, passing on passion from one generation to another is not something that can be taken for granted.

But the tannaitic sage Rabbi Shimon, one of the most important rabbis of his time, to whom the composition of the holy Zohar is attributed, makes a surprising suggestion: "Scripture especially needs to encourage participation in situations in which there is monetary loss" (*Torat Kohanim, Tzav* 1). What this means is the following: The priests would receive portions of meat from most of the sacrifices; at times they alone would have the right to eat them, and at times they were allowed to give them to members of their family. There could be a concern that when a priest would see someone bringing a burnt offering to the Temple, they will say to themselves: "Why should I spend my time offering this sacrifice? I won't get anything out of it!" As a result, they might reject the pilgrim bringing the offering or delay and push him to the end of the line. Therefore, the Torah emphasizes the need to encourage the priests to engage in the work of the sacrifices even when they will not gain anything from it.

This explanation teaches us a fundamental insight into human psychology. People are not angels. They are flesh and blood, even if they work in the Temple and see ten miracles on a daily basis. Even in the place where the Divine Presence resides there is a concern that the priests will prefer those offerings that give them personal benefit.

The Torah's warning is important and necessary not only for priests, but for every person chosen to serve in any position. The word "*kohen*" in Hebrew does not refer to a tribe or a family name; it is first and foremost a job description. God chose particular people to serve, "*lekhahen,*" in the Temple, and therefore, they are called "*kohanim,*" people whose responsibility it is to be dedicated to the form and the essence of their service in the Temple. They need two kinds of encouragement: encouragement to maintain their commitment not only in the first days of service, but for generations to come, and encouragement to provide service to those who come to the Temple, regardless of the personal gain they will or won't derive. People who serve in other capacities, who are also "*kohanim*" in a sense, need encouragement so that they can serve as a voice for those who sent them, and to help each person who turns to them without looking at the benefit they will receive from their efforts on their behalf.

Shemini

Parashat Shemini received its unique name from the first and central section of the portion, which describes the series of events that took place on the eighth day of the consecration of the Tabernacle. Despite extraordinarily high expectations, the day ended in tragedy. Scripture describes at length how, after seven days of preparation and practice, Moses calls Aaron and his four sons and explains to each one what service he will need to perform on the eighth day: who will slaughter the sacrifice, who will throw the blood and where, etc. Initially, everything seems to be proceeding as planned. At the climax of these events, Aaron raises his hands and blesses the people, God's glory manifests, a fire descends from heaven to consume the sacrifice. The nation is inspired, and bows before God, as is said: "And all the people saw it and cried out for joy and threw themselves facedown upon the ground" (9:24).

But here something goes wrong, and the joy is transformed to grief. Aaron's two sons, Nadab and Abihu, bring incense with foreign fire, which they were not commanded to bring, and are then both consumed by fire: "And fire came forth from before the Lord and consumed them and they died" (10:2). Many commentators tried to understand their sin, what motivated them to act in such a manner, and especially why they received such a harsh punishment. We will focus instead on the reactions of Moses and Aaron to this tragedy. Moses, it would seem, tries to offer a theological response to the tragedy: "Of this the Lord spoke when He said: I will be sanctified through those close to Me" (10:3) – an opaque statement that has been interpreted in many ways over the generations. In modern-day Hebrew we might express it like this: God is picking the most beautiful flowers in His garden so as to establish His governance of the world.

Aaron hears what his brother has to say, and prefers not to speak: "And Aaron was silent" (10:3). I have always been impressed not only by the way that Aaron reacts to Moses's words, but even more so that the Torah chooses to record his reaction for us. What hides behind Aaron's silence?

Is it a thunderous silence, or does it express restraint and the desire for understanding? Does it reflect a kind of acceptance of God's judgment, or shock and a sense of impotence? Some of our Sages understood Aaron's silence as his acceptance of the consolation by Moses, who told him that his sons were so righteous and exceptional that God was exceedingly exacting with them, judging their actions with extra stringency.

Others point to the fact that Aaron "was silent" as proof that he wanted to say something, but chose to be silent. What did he want to say? We don't know. It is reasonable to assume that a person in his predicament would want to express anger or frustration, or perhaps criticize God or Moses, who burdened himself and his sons with the responsibility of the priesthood. Perhaps he wanted to raise difficult questions regarding the meaning of such a harsh punishment in the midst of a day of national celebration.

But Aaron chose silence. It was a silence searching for meaning, crying for understanding, but in some hidden place in his heart also accepting that this is a secret that will never be fully understood. This may be the first time that the Torah describes agony and mourning that a person is unable to infuse with meaning. In our limited world, it seems, not everything can be understood in the here and now. Aaron's silence does not necessarily signify comfort; it could very well be that Aaron bore his suffering to the grave. Perhaps what we can hear in Aaron's silence is a call to understand that there isn't always something to be said in every circumstance. Perhaps his silence carries the message that at times, what is needed is to attend to the series of events, from beginning to end, with an understanding that perhaps, in the end, an answer awaits.

Many of our predecessors who survived the horrors of the Holocaust carried impossibly difficult questions with them in their hearts – questions that screamed out to the heavens. This scream, together with the deafening silence of the millions who were murdered, could be heard from one end of the earth to the other. Some of them had a pen and the talent to use it to express their agony and pain; others could only cry bitterly for their most beloved ones who had perished. There were those who turned away from the One whom they expected to help and who didn't provide it. Others were silent, and their silence echoes in the world and shakes the foundations of our human existence. In silence, there is a perspective that seeks to understand and that pursues justice and meaning, but at the same time recognizes our limitations as human beings. In this silence lies the very secret of humanity.

Tazria

Most of the chapters of *Parashat Tazria* discuss different types of leprosy, its diagnosis by the priests, and the process of purification. However, these topics are introduced by another matter entirely.

Parashat Tazria begins with a unique, and somewhat strange law: "If a woman conceives and gives birth to a son, she shall be impure for seven days" (12:2).

We do not fully understand the idea that lies behind the world of purity and impurity. But one principle is very clear: impurity is closely tied to death. A dead body, for example, is considered the "*avi avot,*" the highest super-category of impurity, and anything that touches it becomes an "*av,*" able to spread impurity to other objects. Dead animal carcasses can also defile a person by touch, with a lower level of impurity. As opposed to other religions, which saw death as a symbol of holiness, spirituality, and purity, Judaism saw it as the root of all evil, and the Achilles' heel of the limited physical world. Purity is always connected to life, to a source of living water. Someone who has become impure must immerse in a *mikve* of water in order to return to a state of purity. Indeed, the verse states: "And I will throw pure water upon you." Based on this, a mother who has given birth ought to receive a purity prize, as she brought life into the world, rather than being impure for seven days, just like someone who has touched a dead body! The verses cry out for an explanation.

The Torah also says that every woman who has given birth must bring a sin offering at the end of her period of impurity. This rule also seems exceedingly strange. Usually, a person is required to bring a sin offering after committing sins that, if done intentionally, would warrant a divine death sentence. But here, we are talking about a woman who not only has not sinned, but has done the very opposite. She carried a child in her womb for nine months of pain and effort, and then suffered the pain of labor, thereby enabling the fulfillment of the mitzva to "be fruitful and multiply," and increasing life in the world. Now she is required to bring a sin offering?! Why? What for? What wrong has she committed that she should have to do such a thing?

Our Sages suggest that during her birth pangs, a woman may have made a vow never to give birth again. Since she will certainly not fulfill her vow, she is required to bring a sin offering. This doesn't seem to answer the question precisely, for if this is truly the reason for the offering, we should have to wait to see if she does give birth again, rather than making her bring the offering now, without knowing if she will actually violate her vow.

It seems that the Sages wanted to say that the taking of a vow not to give birth on account of her labor pains is itself the sin, even before the forces of life bring the woman to give birth again.

Bringing a child into the world is not a reason for impurity. Just the opposite: adding life and joy to the world increase purity. But the Torah knew that the process of birth is always accompanied by difficult feelings of weakness, frustration, and pain. There is no such thing as an instant birth. It is a long, exhausting process. We call this weakness and despair – impurity. It takes a great deal of strength to see how a new life that brings blessing to the world can emerge from the place that the woman sits in pain on the birthing stool. Along the way, there is much blood and tears of pain.

The process that brings about the birth of a nation is also preceded by great difficulties. Rabba, one of the greatest rabbis of the talmudic period, who understood what lay in store for us, expressed the harsh statement, "Let it come, and let me not see it," regarding the future redemption (Sanhedrin 98b). If only the day of redemption should come, but I prefer not to see it myself, because of the immense suffering that the process will entail. We are part of the generation in which most people did not themselves experience that most awful of all tragedies; but parents still tell of it, and the live testimonies still reverberate. But our generation has also known its share of suffering – all of the blood that was spilled to establish the State of Israel. At the same time, we are part of the generation that has merited to see the revival of the dry bones, that sees the actualization of the dream of generations before their very eyes. We can remove the feeling of weakness and impurity from ourselves and fulfill the continuation of the verse: "And on the eighth day, the child's foreskin shall be circumcised" (12:3). We, who can already see how the dream is starting to become a reality, can clearly say: "For this child I have prayed." We can all agree that there is still much room for improvement. There is still much inner and outer callousness that we need to remove. But let us not be ingrates. We should be thankful for what we have, and do our best to improve, with God's help, all that needs to be improved.

Metzora

The *parashot* of *Tazria* and *Metzora* tell in great detail of a person who finds signs of disease on his skin or other parts of his body. The verses meticulously describe the symptoms and the ways to become pure. At the end of the *parasha,* we learn that leprosy can afflict not only a person's body, but even his clothing and his house. The moment that signs of leprosy are identified in the house, the priest is called and commanded to take apart the stones in which the leprosy has appeared for a test period. If the phenomenon does not pass, or even spreads, the entire house must be destroyed. This is an unpleasant process. It is not easy to watch the house in which you raised your family being dismantled and broken apart before your eyes. It is reminiscent of the experience of one whose house was razed by a Grad rocket.

But when describing this event, Scripture presents it in an almost festive way, as if it were an event that we were anticipating for years!

This is how the verse reads: "When you enter the land of Canaan that I am giving you as a possession, and I afflict a house in the land you possess with an impure blight" (14:34). It almost sounds as if we have been yearning to enter the Land of Israel just so that we might get leprosy in our house! Isn't this strange?

Our Sages in the Midrash explain that, indeed, there was wonderful news that was buried in the appearance of leprosy in one's house. The previous inhabitants of the land, the Canaanites, had decided to hide their gold and silver in the walls of their house. The Israelites would not have discovered these treasures by natural means. It was only thanks to the leprosy that the opportunity came to discover and benefit from them. This is the reason for the celebratory tone of the opening verse on the topic of house leprosy.

One who reads this midrash surely asks themselves: Was this really the case in every instance of house leprosy? Surely in the second and third generation after coming into the land, all of the treasures had been found already! Moreover, once one or two people discovered the secret of the hidden money in their walls, it's reasonable to assume that everyone else would go and pull up the beams of their floor and take apart their walls in the hopes of hitting the jackpot. And the greatest difficulty with the midrash: Why go to all the trouble of afflicting the house with leprosy? It would have been easier to just tell the people that there may be treasure between their walls, and they would surely look for it themselves.

Rather, it seems that the midrash and the Torah want to offer people a new perspective on troubles that befall us as individuals and as a collective. When something happens that forces us to take apart our home, one can react with stress and hysteria, despair and sadness, and of course, bitterness and anger. Directed against whom? Directed against ourselves, our spouses, our children, or the state. The Torah is teaching us that behind every blight in our home hides a treasure, buried between the walls. The treasure won't always be of gold or silver. It may be a treasure of new insights on life, whose weight and significance are worth many thousands of times more than gold and silver. In our frustration and distress, we don't always have the strength or desire to uncover the treasure, but we should know that it lies there. That doesn't mean that the problem has come on account of the treasure. Nevertheless, it can provide more than a small measure of encouragement and consolation for one who needs to destroy his home.

Our generation is the transitional generation between the tragedy of the Holocaust and the glorious renewal of the Jewish people from the ashes of the ovens of Auschwitz and Majdanek. Even in our generation, we need to continue to search for the treasures that are found between the walls. This does not offer any explanation or justification for the horrors. But the treasure of souls found between the ovens and the mass graves is the flowing spring that nourishes the roots of our existence here in the Jewish state. The souls of our brethren oblige us to ensure that Jewish identity continues throughout the generations. They cry out to us to listen to all that they represented in their lives and in their deaths. Millions of our people who were murdered left us, in their writings, their life stories, and their heroism, spiritual treasures with the power to light our paths for generations to come.

Aḥarei Mot

Parashat Aḥarei Mot begins with a discussion of the service of the high priest on Yom Kippur, followed by an extensive presentation of forbidden sexual unions. At the end of this section, the Torah adds a recommendation and a warning:

> Do not make yourselves impure in any of these ways, for it is by all these that the nations I am casting out before you made themselves impure. And so the land itself became impure, and I held it to account for its sins, and the land vomited out its inhabitants.... The people who lived in the land before you committed all these abhorrent acts and the land became impure. Let

> the land not vomit you out for making it impure, as it vomited out the nation there before you. (18:24–28)

Scripture connects illicit sexual relations with the possibility of exile from the land. The language it uses is harsh: the land "vomits." This is not merely exile, but expulsion outward. What is the connection between these two topics? Why is a healthy and stable family the basis for our inheritance of the land, while weakening the family unit leads to being uprooted from the land, according to the biblical perspective?

It seems that the Torah is seeking to set a new standard for a people looking to build its national home. The foundations of the nation will not be based in hatred of the other (even if he is hostile), nor in shirt and scarf in the colors of our favorite soccer team (although they raise spirits and create a feeling of togetherness). A healthy nation will be founded on small social circles with high levels of solidarity. First among them is the small and powerful family unit. A nation cannot be disconnected from what is going on in the smaller units from which it is constituted. Even during the Exodus, we were informed that the celebration of independence from Egypt would not start on a stage with musicians and choirs, but rather with intimate family rituals which would allow for conversation between parent and child – a conversation about what happened in Egypt, and what is happening to us now. Applying this idea to our times, and the celebration of our own independence in this generation, would suggest that we should use the day to tell our children about what was here before Herzl and before the state was established. Who were the *maapilim*? What was illegal resistance? Why is the state critical for our survival?

The Torah speaks of "a lamb for his family, one for *every household*" (Exodus 12:3). The barbecue of the Paschal sacrifice was performed among family because that is where national redemption begins. This motif continues in the verses in our *parasha*. The Torah's warnings about the need to be stringent regarding the proper family structure seeks to convey the message that national solidarity depends on the solidarity of the family unit.

The Torah's verses sound an important alarm. We cannot take our presence in this land as an irreversible reality. We are right to celebrate the state's glorious achievements. The establishment of the state was an important stage in an ongoing series of activities that spanned decades: conquering the desolation of the land, draining the swamps, settlement in swaths of land that people hadn't walked for hundreds of years, and above all, the miracle of the ingathering of the exiles who came from all corners of the earth after two thousand years of exile and suffering. Less than a century after the great tragedy of our people, we can be proud of our success in building an impressive economy and a strong army. These are both critically important in creating the infrastructure for the physical well-being of the state. They are necessary conditions, but not sufficient ones. Everyone knows that a strong army needs appropriate equipment to succeed in its missions. But an army lacking morale, motivation, and the understanding of what it is fighting for and why will not succeed. A soldier who doesn't understand why it's important to be part of this nation and this state will ask himself if it isn't better to seek his future elsewhere. He will seek to avoid military service in general, and certainly meaningful service. If we will not succeed in offering a model of a society with profound moral fortitude, we will have a hard time maintaining a state in the long run. A society in which no one helps as a person bleeds to death will have a hard time exhibiting solidarity when rockets fall on Sderot and Netivot. A society in which violence has become a national plague that can break out for trivial reasons, like a fight over parking or a soccer game, will have a hard time uniting when it counts.

The *parasha* can be understood as a religious warning regarding divine reward and punishment. But in my opinion, one who understands it that way may miss the main point.

This isn't a narrative about punishment, but a deep understanding of the human psyche. For a society to survive in this land, it needs people infused with a belief in the sanctity of life, both private and national. It needs people who recognize that our national spirit will be built based on the way that we sanctify our personal lives. Our own pleasure is not illegitimate, but is a part of a much larger network of social values to which we are meant to be committed.

Kedoshim

The *parashot* of *Aḥarei Mot* and *Kedoshim* are adjacent to one another, and are sometimes read together, as if they were one *parasha*. Nonetheless, there is a significant difference between them, both in style and content. *Aḥarei Mot* focuses on two main topics – the service of the high priest on Yom Kippur, and the prohibitions regarding illicit sexual unions. *Parashat Kedoshim,* on the other hand, contains discussions of a wide variety of topics that do not seem at all related to one another. More than fifty positive and negative commandments are mentioned in the *parasha*. Some of them are between man and God, like the sanctity and observance of Shabbat and prohibitions against idol worship; some are between man and his fellow, like respecting one's parents and the elderly ("Stand before the elderly"; 19:32) and the prohibition against cursing a deaf person or placing a stumbling block before a blind person.

It is hard to understand what connects the mitzva to honor one's parents to the requirement to leave a corner of your field to the poor; what connects the prohibition against delaying a worker's payment and the prohibition against turning to idols. Over the years, many and varied attempts were made to find the thread that runs through all of these laws. I want to examine two social mitzvot that we encounter very frequently. They are mentioned next to one another in one verse, even though there seems to be little connection between them. The verse says: "Do not go around as a gossipmonger among your people, do not stand by while your neighbor's life is in danger; I am the Lord" (19:16).

The first part of the verse commands us not to spread gossip. We all know exactly what this means, but what is the halakhic definition of gossiping? It actually includes a number of types of "gossipmongering"; one of them is revealing secrets about one's friend that may hurt that person (leaks from government or committee meetings are included in this prohibition). It also includes something that one person said about another, but did not intend for that person to hear.

The second part of the verse commands us not to be

a bystander when someone else is in danger. This mitzva applies whether the danger is a physical one, as when a person is drowning or was in an accident, or financial, as when a person is liable to lose money in a fraudulent business deal or because a company is on the verge of collapse. Both of these laws are very clear, on their own, but what is the connection between the parts of the verse? These would seem to be totally distinct mitzvot. Moreover, why does the Torah add the words "I am the Lord" to the end of the verse?

One of the most important principles in the life of a society is the need to balance between different values, each of which is correct in its own right, but which sometimes contradict one another when it comes to practice. The idea that we are people who make value decisions means, first and foremost, that we understand the need to balance between values when they clash. If I know, for example, that the person with whom my friend is about to go into business is a fraud, should I tell him this? If my friend is driving with impaired vision, will I report him to the licensing authorities? On the one hand, there is the strict prohibition against gossiping. I don't want to speak negatively about my friend. On the other hand, if the good of the community, or an individual who will be hurt, is considered, I must warn everyone who might be affected of a possible danger. In every society, there will be those who try to avoid any involvement with the excuse that they don't want to speak gossip, and this is precisely why the Torah warns us that one who acts thus, and allows their fellow to be hurt, is at risk of violating a prohibition just as severe. To make a decision in these situations is complex, and many people struggle with the question when to reveal and when to hide. The Torah finishes with the words "I am the Lord," as if to say that only the One who can read our thoughts and feelings knows whether our speech and our silence come from pure motivations and an interest to repair. One of the constant challenges of any society is how to create a supportive, caring community that doesn't ignore what is going on within it, or shirk responsibility but, on the other hand, is not invasive and gossipy; a caring and sensitive society, but one that is also enabling and inclusive.

Emor

The first part of the book of Leviticus discusses the sanctity of the Tabernacle and the sacrifices, and describes the priestly service in detail, and is therefore referred to as "*Torat Kohanim*," the "Instruction of the Priests." *Parashat Emor* introduces a new dimension into the world of sanctity – the dimension of time.

An entire chapter is dedicated to the Jewish festivals – the three pilgrimage festivals, Rosh HaShana, and Yom Kippur. For the most part, each holiday has a set date that is mentioned explicitly. For example, the first of Tishrei is Rosh HaShana, the tenth of Tishrei is Yom Kippur, and so it goes for Passover and Sukkot. But the situation is entirely different with regard to Shavuot. This holiday has no date: we are meant to reach it by counting. We are commanded to count forty-nine days from the second day of Passover, and to celebrate Shavuot on the fiftieth day. In the past, the holiday could actually fall out on different dates, based on the question of when the court sanctified the month of Sivan, but always forty-nine days after the second day of Passover. These days are known as "*Sefirat HaOmer*," named for the Omer sacrifice brought on the second day of Passover. We count from that day until we reach Shavuot. In a later time, 24,000 students of Rabbi Akiva died during this period, apparently in the Bar Kokhba rebellion. When the Torah was given, however, these days of counting were not days of mourning. Just the opposite – they were joyous days of preparation for the holiday of Shavuot.

The difference between Shavuot and other holidays demands an explanation. Why does every other holiday have a date, and only Shavuot is reached by counting? We are familiar with the idea of a "countdown" in our lives: children count down the days until school is over and vacation begins; soldiers count down the days until they finish their mandatory service; and when a rocket is launched, there is a countdown to launch.

But we need to distinguish between different types of countings. Some countings don't demand anything beyond themselves. Time does the work, and you just need to watch passively, wondering when the thing that needs to happen will actually happen. But there is a counting that is meant to tell us that an important event is about to happen, but that it won't happen on its own: we need to prepare for it. Such is the countdown to launch, or the countdown to a military operation.

In general, Passover was based on divine acts, on miracles and wonders. But these cannot replace the human spirit, that needs to build itself and its world. If a person wants to receive the Torah, if a person wants to grow spiritually, he must count by himself. He must exert his own efforts, and only then can he reach any kind of spiritual perfection. It is impossible to move from Passover to Shavuot, the festival of receiving the Torah, without appropriate human efforts, expressed by the counting.

These are days of song and praise for the human need to exert effort in order to build his spiritual world. Over time, some things in the Jewish people went awry. Our Sages tell us that all of Rabbi Akiva's students died during this counting period because they did not treat one another with respect. Disrespecting others is not a one-time event, but an ongoing behavior that presumably took place during other days of the year as well, and not just these. But perhaps it is specifically during this period, when we are meant to be working on our spiritual refinement, that if people insult one another instead, the human spirit is utterly demeaned. When this happens, the days of joyous counting become days of mourning.

This was true in those days, and it remains true at this time. Every nation that enjoys political independence has the right and the duty to decide on its political and social policies. Every time this right and duty is actualized, it is a celebration of the human spirit that seeks to convince others of the righteousness of its path. But the celebration turns into tragedy when the way that this is done is by demeaning the other.

Behar

If I were asked what *parasha* in the Torah is most concerned with "social justice," I wouldn't hesitate for a moment before answering. If there is one place that has an intense, systematic focus on social questions it is *Parashat Behar*. The *parasha* surveys the laws of the *Shemitta* year, in which all produce of the fields and the trees are declared ownerless, and the laws of the Jubilee year, in which lands that had been sold return to their original owner and slaves are freed to return home after years of hard work far from their families. The verses of the *parasha* discuss various circumstances of distress that people may face in their lives and explain how to cope with these circumstances.

In the midst of all this, the Torah commands us to

act fairly in our business dealings: "But when you sell land to your fellow or buy it from him, brother must not cheat brother" (25:14). The Torah repeats this same command twice in the same chapter, in verse 14 and verse 17, and this led the Sages to imbue the word "cheating" (*honaa*) with two separate meanings. The simple explanation of the word is not to lie or deceive in business dealings. It is forbidden to sell a damaged or used item under the pretense that it is pristine or new. But the Sages added another meaning to this command, that it is forbidden to cause another person distress. To make their intentions even more clear, they brought a number of examples: If someone asks where they can buy something, it is forbidden to deceive them and send them to the wrong place. It is even forbidden to give a seller the impression that we're interested in buying something that we have no intention to purchase (because of the disappointment this will cause them; see Bava Metzia 58b).

The prohibition against causing another person pain or distress is one of the most challenging laws in the Torah. It is easy to understand that murder, theft, or rape are heinous deeds that have no place in civilized society. It is much more difficult to internalize that deception, or the habit of putting other people down, can destroy the fabric of society in similar ways.

People only rarely deteriorate to the point of committing grave sins; most normative people do not undertake those actions at all. Our quality of life is much more affected by the small stabbing pains that we cause our neighbors or friends. It can take place at any time and any place – in a fight over parking spots in a crowded lot, if we cut someone in a line at the supermarket, when teenagers make noise late into the night in a quiet, suburban neighborhood. It is precisely within the *parasha* that speaks about the foundations of the proper social order that God takes the trouble to remind us that before we go out to repair the whole world and overcome the tycoons and all those who oppress the worker, we need to make the necessary repairs within our own home, in the way we treat our partner, our children, and our neighbors.

Israeli society as a whole is always horrified to hear of terrible acts of murder, like the story of the man who was stabbed to death simply because he had the audacity to tell a group of youths to stop making so much noise, so that his baby daughter could sleep. It is just and proper to be horrified by such a meaningless, senseless murder. But too quickly, we return to the status quo regarding the setting of this tragedy: the noise itself and the willingness to disturb the sleep of one's neighbors. We have accepted the fact that it is fine to make noise, even if it prevents others from sleeping. We have become accustomed to this happening, saying: "This is our youth these days, and there's nothing we can do about it!"

The foundational tenet that Hillel taught the non-Jew who wanted to convert was: "What is hateful to you, do not do to your fellow" (Shabbat 31a). All the rest of the Torah is simply commentary to this tenet, and the explanations of how to practice it.

Our children are not any worse than us. They want to learn from us, as long as we speak in a clear voice, and act in accordance with it. We need to put a stop to *honaa* in all its forms, to end deception, and end the causing of distress.

Beḥukkotai

Beḥukkotai is the final *parasha* in the book of Leviticus, and in its center is the section of the "rebuke."

The "rebuke" is essentially a synonym for the contract made between God and the nation, according to which if the people follow the Torah's laws and values, they will enjoy financial comfort and security. If, God forbid, they act in the opposite way, they will face a period of financial difficulty and security woes, until the point of total destruction. One of the most idyllic promises made is: "I will grant peace in the land; when you lie down, no one will make you afraid… and through that land no sword shall pass" (26:6). There is a certain stylistic difficulty with the verse. After all, if there is peace in the land, and no one needs to be afraid, why mention the fact that the sword shall not pass through the land? If no one is fighting, of course there is no need for swords.

Some of the commentators explained that the verse means that regional peace will be so stable that nations will not need to pass our land on their way to battle others. But if this is the explanation, this verse would seem to hold no blessing for us. Others explained that people bearing swords will not be allowed to enter the state; but this seems like security advice, rather than a blessing. Perhaps we can explain that the verse promises us that not only will we have peace from our external enemies, but even our swords that are pointed at one another will no longer pass through the land; the culture of the Sicarii will disappear from the land.

From the dawn of our national life, the question of internal security was no less critical than the question of external security. During the Second Temple period, it was the Sicarii, the people of the knife, who bore responsibility for the Temple's destruction no less than the Romans who besieged the city from without. The swords that still circulate among us in our land seem to threaten our security today no less than the Iranian threat. If young men and women are afraid to go out into the streets of the first great Hebrew city for fear of what will happen, we need to engage in a profound self-reckoning. Of course, it's possible to take the easy way out and to blame the police for its impotence in facing growing waves of crime. If only they had acted with greater zeal and reacted on time, lives would have been saved. It may be that this criticism has some truth to it. Greater police presence in places of recreation in city centers could well deter violent criminals and prevent severe actions.

But even if there is truth to this criticism, it only relates to the symptom, and not to the essence of the problem. In the section of the rebuke when the Torah wants to describe going in the wrong direction, it uses the words "And if you walk contrary (*keri*) to Me" (26:21). *Keri* means in happenstance, that is, when we see that there are terrible plagues being meted out to us, we will think that it is only happenstance, only coincidental. The worst curse for a person is a situation in which he cannot assign any meaning to the events that happen to him and with which he must cope.

Violence is not divinely decreed, and the solution to it does not only lie in the hands of the police. The police have an important role in creating deterrence and in punishment, but they cannot quash the desire to do crime. Coping with violence starts in the home, in the playground, and in the schools. We must clarify to ourselves and to our children that there are some means that should never be used, even when we are very angry and hurt. We must learn that it is possible and necessary to control our desire for immediate satisfaction at any cost. This is true when we are dealing with a child demanding an expensive phone, or a candy that they wanted. If we can restrain our child's need for immediate satisfaction, as well as our own (avoiding confrontation by buying their quiet), we will move ourselves and our children to a place of greater self-control and significant social improvement. When we teach our children that violence is not an option, there will be almost no need at all for the police.

POCKET

Numbers

במדבר

Bemidbar

Parashat Bemidbar lends its name to the book of *Bemidbar* as a whole. It is a fitting name not only because the word "*bemidbar*," "in the desert," appears in the first verse of the book, but primarily because the central topic of the fourth book of the Torah is the journey of the Israelites in the desert during their forty-year period of wandering. We almost always begin reading the book of *Bemidbar* adjacent to the holiday of Shavuot. This would seem not to be a coincidence; the Torah, of course, was given in the Sinai desert.

One of the mysteries that perplexed the Sages was the location of the giving of the Torah. The desert can be an awe-inspiring place, but it is also usually far from settled areas and necessary sources of water. Would it not have been more appropriate to hold this unprecedented, historic moment in a somewhat more honorable and worthy place?

The midrashim offer different answers to this question. There are those that say that the reason behind the divine decision to give the Torah in the desert was "so as not to leave room for the nations to claim: 'We did not accept the Torah because it was given in their land.'" God did not want to give the nations of the world an excuse to justify their refusal to receive the Torah. Were it to have been given in Israel, they could excuse themselves by saying that the Torah was given in the sovereign territory of another nation. Other sages say that the reason for choosing the desert was "so that there not be disagreement among the tribes, that one would say, 'It was given in my land,' and the other would say, 'It was given in my land.'" God knows the Jewish people and their internecine bickering well. If the Torah had been given in a particular place, a civil world war between different groups would have broken out, with each one claiming ownership of the Torah. The Midrash summarizes the different reasons: "For this reason, the Torah was given in the desert…an ownerless place. The Torah was given with three things, with desert, with fire, and with water, to teach us: Just as these are free for all the world's inhabitants, so too are the words of Torah free for all the world's inhabitants" (*Mekhilta DeRabbi Yishmael, Masekhta DeBaḥodesh, Yitro* 5).

The words of the Midrash need no further explanation. The Torah was given in a place in which no group or body could claim ownership over it. The logical extension of this is the following: The organizing principle of the desert is that no group has any formal ownership over it, but there are still those who ultimately have more power and influence over it. Whoever actually spends time in the desert, who knows all its wadis, who ascends its cliffs and descends into its streams, is the one who will be king of the desert. The desert is an ownerless territory, but it can be acquired through blood, sweat, and tears.

So too is the Torah. It is also only acquired by one who "kills themselves in the tent of Torah." As the Sages said: "If a person does not make himself as ownerless as the desert, he will not merit acquiring the Torah" (*Yalkut Shimoni, Yitro* 273). If we want to connect to the wonderful world of Torah and wisdom, we need to invest effort. Only in this way will we make it our inheritance.

Naso

Parashat Naso is the longest *parasha* in the Torah: 176 verses. There are many topics in the *parasha,* and they are not all connected to one another. One of the unique subjects that is discussed is the law of the *sota,* the wife suspected of adultery. The Torah describes a situation in which a man is jealous and demands of his wife not to be alone with another man, and she does not listen to him. The husband suspects that his wife cheated on him, while she denies everything. He brings her to the Temple and she is required to drink special waters that are meant to test whether or not she was faithful. The process of preparing the water is explained in detail. The *kohen* would put ashes into them, as well as a piece of parchment upon which were written verses from the Torah concerning the laws of the *sota*. The water erases the letters on the parchment, including God's name; and this is what the woman is meant to drink.

The process seems exceedingly strange. In Jewish law, as in any other legal system, there are generally clear principles for how a person can be convicted in a criminal or civil case. Here, for some reason, Scripture involves divine measures in the resolution of a marital dispute. Indeed, rabbis throughout the generations noted the singularity of this topic. For example, the Ramban (twelfth century) writes, in his commentary on the Torah: "There is nothing that depends on a miracle in all of the Torah's laws except this" (Numbers 5:20–21). Hence we must ask: Why did the Torah make this matter different than all others? Why did it demand that we act differently regarding marital loyalty and betrayal than every other legal matter?

There is a verse in Song of Songs that describes a woman's desire to be the center of her lover's attention with the following words: "Set me like a seal upon your heart, like the seal upon your arm – for love is as powerful as death itself, and jealousy unyielding as Sheol" (8:6). Relationships between lovers are characterized by high levels of sensitivity and concern, appreciation and openness, but at the same time they can transform in a moment into enmity and jealousy, suspicion and apathy. The emotions that lead to endless sacrifice on behalf of one's partner can bring a night later to murder. That is the world of love and lovers. Powerful as death, unyielding as Sheol.

The root of the crisis and the solution lie in one word: trust. Trust is built over time by actions and words, but it is more than the sum of the actions and words that built it; it is a fundamental feeling that a person has toward their partner. Trust in love, trust that my loved one won't hurt me, trust that they want what is best for me. The trust that partners build in one another is one of the fundamental building blocks of society. If lovers can't trust one another, how can a child trust his parents? How can a worker and an employer, or a soldier and a commander, trust one another? It's hard to imagine an army in which a soldier would demand to receive every order in writing, to protect himself from the possibility that a commander will deny that he gave a certain command (which does happen occasionally). The same goes for family relationships.

If the framework of trust between partners, the basis of their relationship, is so damaged that a husband suspects his wife of cheating on him, the covenant between them has apparently reached a point at which repairing it cannot rely on legal, technical mechanisms. What is needed is a treatment at the root of the problem, and this is the divine intervention of the *sota* waters.

This root treatment can work when most people in society trust one another; although trust may be violated by a small minority, it is still considered the natural and desired state of affairs. If trust stops being a significant value in our lives, the miraculous water won't help. Our Sages said regarding this: "When adulterers multiplied, the waters of the *sota* were annulled." A society that has lost its respect for trust and the loyalty that builds it, a society in which betrayal and mistrust are common, cannot be helped by root treatments in specific cases, even if it is a miraculous message from God. The root treatment needed by such a society is a much more comprehensive educational process.

The *parasha* of *sota* calls on us to return trust as the foundation of our relationships with our partners, our children, and all those who surround us.

Behaalotekha

Parashat Behaalotekha is named for the command given to Aaron to ascend the steps of the Menora, the candelabrum in the Temple, on a daily basis in order to light it. The celebratory tone of the beginning of the *parasha* holds no hint of what will happen at its end.

After the verses describe in detail the way that the camp will travel in the desert, the great day finally arrives on which the Jewish people begin their journey to the Land of Israel. The historic date is the twentieth of Iyar, the second year after the Exodus. A journey that was meant to take only a few days suffers one setback after another, until finally becoming a forty-year sojourn in the desert.

The first problem is described in the following words:

"The people began to rail bitterly in the Lord's presence" (11:1). The simple explanation of the term "*mitonenim*" is to complain. At this stage, Scripture doesn't mention the nature of the people's complaint, and many commentaries try to understand its content. There were sages who said that the people complained that they wanted to worship idols as they had become accustomed to doing in Egypt, something which had now been strictly forbidden. But there is no hint of this in the verses. Moreover, this story happens almost a year after the giving of the Torah and the sin of the Golden Calf. Did they only remember to complain now that they were prohibited from worshipping idols? It would seem that we should search for a solution elsewhere.

Perhaps the Jewish people complained about setting off on their journey. Mount Sinai, where they had encamped for almost a year, was relatively close to civilization. Once they depart from it, the fears about the difficulties of the journey and the suffering caused by traveling in the sweltering desert heat increased. After spending almost a year in one place, no one wanted to give up on the temporary rest they had been enjoying to set out on a long, frightening journey. Other commentaries suggested that the word "*mitonenim*" comes from the root of "*aninut*," meaning pain and mourning. According to this interpretation, the verse is suggesting that the people were hurting and sad; but the reason for this pain remains unclear.

It could be that a single word, or, in fact, a single letter, could lend a new meaning to the entire story. The Torah does not simply say that they were complaining, "*mitonenim,*" but that they were "*kemitonenim,*" they were *like* complainers. If the Torah wanted to speak about the nation's complaint, it would have described its content, as it does in other cases. But Scripture wants to offer a different perspective on this event. The Israelites, in fact, had nothing to complain about; they had everything they needed. A well of water accompanied them wherever they turned. They were provided with food on a regular, dependable basis. The nation was organized by tribe, with a stunning Tabernacle in the camp's center, and they were guided by a pillar of cloud and fire, which also protected them from enemies. What could be bad? What were they missing? But people have an easier time complaining about what they lack than appreciating what they have. It's easier to express pain and anger than to express contentment and to happily accept everything that one receives. We take the good for granted and enjoy complaining about what is bad. Therefore, the verse says that they were *like* complainers. There is no reason to search for the nature of the complaint, because there actually wasn't one. It was complaining for its own sake.

Rashi described it in this way: "They were looking for a reason to separate themselves from God." People look for reasons to complain in order to justify inappropriate behavior and estrangement from God that has no real reason. The Torah does not deny that there are times that criticism and repair are needed. However, it is always worthwhile to ask whether the complaint comes to truly repair and build, or whether it is purely for the sake of complaining. This complaint, at the very beginning of the journey in the desert, can help us think about our complaints about ourselves and our children throughout our lives. It's not a good idea to make complaining a way of life.

Shelaḥ

At the center of *Parashat Shelaḥ* is the story of the spies whom Moses sends to survey the Land of Israel, to evaluate the quality of its fruit and the nature of its inhabitants. Scripture tells how the spies return from the Promised Land, bringing large fruits, which bear a clear message: the land flows with milk and honey. We are all familiar with the picture: two people carrying a huge bunch of grapes on their shoulders using a pole, as the verse says: "Which they carried on a pole between two men" (13:23). This image became the symbol of the bounty of the land; Israeli vineyards, as well as Israeli tour companies, use it as their logo.

But there is one very small problem: It will be difficult to conquer the land because of the powerful nations that live in it. Regarding this, the spies make the crushing statement: "We cannot go up against those people, for they are stronger than us" (13:31). Not everyone agrees with this evaluation; Caleb the son of Jephunneh says authoritatively: "Let us go up at once and take possession of it" (13:30). The dispute becomes increasingly heated until the spies declare that it is a land "that consumes its inhabitants" (13:32). The people are convinced by the opinion of the majority of the spies and complain about Moses's plan to bring them to the land. Joshua and Caleb make a supreme effort to convince the people that the land is good, and that with God's help, they will be able to conquer it, but for nought. When the Jewish people raise their voices and cry that night, refusing to enter the land, God decides that all those who spoke out against the land will not merit to enter it. Rather, their punishment will be to wander for forty years, until the generation has died out.

Why was such a harsh punishment chosen? Can't people make a mistake in their evaluation and think that it is dangerous to enter the land under certain circumstances? Wasn't it reasonable of the nation to listen to the majority opinion of the spies who claimed that it was not worthwhile to try to enter the land? Is God so angry that the Jewish people don't trust Him?

One of the phrases in the *parasha* can give us a hint

that will help us understand this. "Those men who spoke ill of the land died" (14:37). The word "*dibba*," "speech," appears a number of times, as if that were the problem. What does the land care if they spoke ill of it? Is it a person who feels and is hurt by slander?

The Torah here teaches us a basic principle of behavior. It is fine to argue and to criticize, but it is forbidden to slander. The land will not be hurt by criticism, but we will all be hurt if this toxicity is put out into the world. The very air we breathe is polluted by the atmosphere of slander and verbal abuse.

It could be that Scripture is teaching us an even more difficult lesson to digest. Since our earliest days as a people, there were those who reviled the land and looked for any excuse to disconnect from it. Sometimes these were excuses related to security, and sometimes they were related to various ideological claims. There were those who claimed that we should integrate with the non-Jews, others who said that we should not move to Israel because of the difficulty of observing mitzvot there, etc. Different reasons, but their common denominator is their bottom line: to remain in exile. Rabbi Yehuda HaLevi, one of the greatest medieval Jewish thinkers, called this phenomenon a disgrace when he said: "You have found the place of my disgrace, king of Kuzar." It is a disgrace to pray three times a day to return to Jerusalem, and yet remain in Spain or Poland or the United States. Chapter 106 of Psalms, which reviews the sojourn of Israel in the desert, summarizes it with the words: "They spurned the most desirable land" (106:24). It could be that there was merit to some of the claims made against connecting to the land; but in the end, those who cleave to the land will merit to see it and connect to it along with the Jewish people throughout history. Those who spurn it will remain in the desert.

The Zionist movement is a direct continuation of those giants (like the Vilna Gaon and his students) whose entire desire was to reconnect to the Land of Israel. True, there are arguments regarding its path, but one cannot take away the merit due for its role in establishing the state and the important part it played in settling the land. This movement is the greatest repair of the sin of the spies. Of course, its successes were anathema to those who wanted to continue to spurn the "most desirable land." But the lovers of the land, even when they disagree with the Zionist movement on small or large details, remember that the land "flows with milk and honey." If we can only remember the One who allowed us to inherit the land, and remember not to spurn this treasure, we will merit to fulfill the words of Caleb: "Let us go up at once and take possession of it."

Koraḥ

Parashat Koraḥ is one of the more famous *parashot* in the Torah, and has provided endless fodder for rabbinic homilies and explanations throughout the generations. To a great extent, the *parasha* offers a distillation of Jewish history throughout time, along with all the components of a great story: arguments, disputes, and juicy politics. The main storyline concerns a group that sought to undermine Moses's leadership: "All the community is holy.... Why do you set yourselves above the Lord's people?" (16:3). It's a classic, common scene in the world of politics – the group that seeks to overthrow the current leader with various complaints. The modern response to these complaints is usually to go to primaries, or some other democratic process. In the ancient world, the standard response was to decapitate the leaders of the rebellion (a policy that can still be witnessed in various countries in our own day). Moses's response to the claims of Korah and his people is surprising. Initially, he suggests that everyone making a claim to the priesthood should bring incense before God. The offering that God accepts will attest to the chosen leader. In a later stage of the rebellion, the tone changes. Moses lets the people know that he will be satisfied with nothing less than the death of those who arose against him. But not just with any death. He demands of God that the earth should open its mouth and swallow all of the rebels. If this miraculous, extraordinary punishment does not befall them, it will be absolute proof that Moses is indeed not the chosen leader. Moses's demand was met; the earth opened its mouth and swallowed Korah and his company, along with their houses and property.

The story raises many questions. Why is the way that his opponents will die critically important to Moses? Why does Moses, who spent his life entreating God to forgive sinners, suddenly change his tune here and ask God not to listen to them or accept their offerings?

In the history of our people, as in the history of other peoples, many leaders were raised aloft by waves of populism that swept up the masses. The nature of populism is the appeal to people's lowest emotions, to rally them to the benefit of the leader, who uses every opportunity to increase his power and standing. In some places, leaders rode waves of xenophobia, emphasizing a unifying ethnic and national identity. In other places, they used the love of money to incite a war of social and economic classes, promising equality in the division of resources, while creating the illusion that this was possible in the short term.

What person with low socioeconomic standing wouldn't dream of enjoying equal conditions with the rich man, and what citizen doesn't lean towards seeing the stranger as someone who threatens his status, and therefore who ought to be dealt with? Everyone is holy, everyone deserves the same property, and the human imagination readily sympathizes with other "everyone" claims. Korah and his company sought to ride the wave of public sentiment that there should be no hierarchy in the world, that everyone is exactly the same.

True, all are equal before God, but that doesn't mean that everyone can be priests in the Temple. God does not reject anyone's prayer, but that doesn't mean that everyone can lead the prayer. Everyone has the right to dignity, life, and livelihood, but that doesn't mean that everyone can be a pilot or a doctor; one who learned and trained themselves for the position can accept the appropriate responsibility. Every person with any health problem deserves to be treated fairly and with respect, but that doesn't mean that we'll recruit them to serve in an elite army unit.

Moses seeks to teach the people a lesson in true leadership. He is not only interested in getting rid of those who rebelled. If that were the case, we would be dealing with just another leader seeking power. Moses asks God to create something new, that the earth should open its mouth and swallow those who claim that everyone is holy. He wants to say: We don't live in that kind of world. In a utopian world, we would expect that there would be no differences between people – not economic, social, or physical. But in the complex world in which we live, we need to recognize that different people receive different talents, and everyone must maximize them to the best of their abilities.

One can claim that every human being deserves to live with dignity, and that we need to do the utmost to treat every person in a warm, loving manner. But at the same time, we need to recognize that, ultimately, Jewish society cannot maintain its identity without distinguishing between ourselves and those who are not part of us. One can claim that everyone needs to contribute to the economic and security needs of the state – this is correct. But one who thinks that can be achieved by destroying all existing frameworks and definitions all at once is mistaken and misleads others. Statements like "We are all the same" are fundamentally correct, but are difficult, or perhaps even impossible, to actualize immediately in our complex world. We need to progress, but patiently. Not to give up, but to act moderately.

Ḥukkat

Chronologically speaking, most of the events in *Parashat Ḥukkat* take place after forty years of wandering, toward the end of the Jewish people's journey in the desert. The *parasha* presents us with a number of exceptionally dramatic stories: the death of Aaron and Miriam, the encounter between the Israelites and nations that do not allow them to pass through their borders or help them with provisions, the events which determined that Moses and Aaron would not be allowed to enter the Land of Israel, and more. But the *parasha* doesn't begin with any of these dramatic events. The first topic that it discusses is the laws of the red heifer – the process required to prepare the purifying waters, and the way to become pure. The words that open up the topic are: "This is the statute of the Torah" (19:2), which begs the exegetical question: Why didn't the Torah state: "This is the statute of the heifer"? After all, this section discusses the laws of the red heifer, not of the Torah as a whole.

Moreover, a person who touches a dead body is defined as ritually impure for seven days. During this period, they may not enter the Temple or consume any sacrifices offered there. One returns to a state of purity when water mixed with the ashes of the red heifer are sprinkled on him, on the third and seventh day of his defilement. The heifer had to have exceedingly rare coloring – completely red, without any black hairs. It also needed to be a cow that had never borne any kind of yoke. This is not an easy requirement to meet in a land where the main work animals are oxen. Hence these animals were extremely rare, and their cost was astronomical. Our Sages recount that over the course of hundreds of years that the Jewish people lived in its land, a red heifer was found and slaughtered to prepare its ashes only seven times.

Someone reading about this process for the first time certainly wonders: What is this all about? But even someone who reads it every year has a hard time explaining these laws. What is all this meant to be? What is the purpose of the ashes? Why specifically a heifer, why does it need to red, and why does it need to be one that was never worked?

It shouldn't trouble us if we haven't yet understood how and why this works. After all, this is one of the most exceptional laws in the Torah, which our Sages called a "*ḥok*" – a principle etched in stone, a divine decision that transcends human understanding. Nevertheless, we will try to understand some of what lies beneath this mysterious *parasha*.

Two rabbinic midrashim shed new light on the topic of the red heifer. In one of them, the Sages ask: "Why do all the sacrifices come from male animals, and this comes from a female animal?" Their answer: "It can be compared to the son of a maidservant who soiled the king's palace. The king said: Let his mother come and clean up the excrement. So did God say: Let the cow come to atone for the sin of the calf" (Numbers Rabba 19:8). According to this midrash, the burning of the red heifer is somehow connected to the sin of the Golden Calf and to the defilement that it caused. The red cow is meant to clean up for that failure. How so? What is the connection between the two, other than the interesting fact that the cow is indeed the mother of the calf?

A different midrash offers another explanation: "Why a red cow? To atone for the red sin that they made a golden calf, and not only that sin was red, but indeed, all sins are red, therefore the cow must be red. And when she is burned, her ash is white, as it says: 'Though your sins be like scarlet, they will grow whiter than snow' (Isaiah 1:18)" (midrashim from Geniza manuscripts, 2:86).

Both midrashim are emphasizing the same point. The sin of the Golden Calf, the first sin after the giving of the Torah, is the prototype for all sins. Therefore, it serves as a model for all of humanity's failures. The essence of the failure lies in clinging to the physical world of the senses: "These are your gods, Israel" (Exodus 32:4), cried the people, pointing their fingers at the golden calf. The desire to cling to the physical can create the illusion that that is what exists and what is important in the world, while the world of the spirit and the soul is merely imaginary. The encounter with death can intensify this feeling; facing death, a person senses the transience of the physical world. He may tend to think, God forbid, that the material world is the foundation of existence, and that without it, the world ceases to have any meaning. The Torah seeks to root out the feeling of nothingness created in the meeting with death; this is the essence of "impurity." The laws of the red heifer demonstrate that failure in this world is the result of sin. Eternal life exists in a person's values, in his soul, and in the image of God that exists in each of us. Burning the red and turning it white reminds humanity that we can fix our failures. This won't help prevent death, but it will make one's spiritual life an eternal one.

Therefore, the *parasha* begins: "This is the statute of the Torah." This is not merely another verse about the red heifer. We are really talking about the essence of a person's life. Does he allow the "red," the material, to dominate him, or does he realize that he is part of the world of eternal values of the Jewish people and of God's spirit that was embedded in every person? Is he limited to the short timespan of his body's life, or does this spirit allow him to aspire to the good, the just, and to eternity itself?

Balak

Balak is the name of Moab's king, through whose land the Israelites were meant to pass on their way to Israel. Concerned that they will damage his land as they pass through, he decides, rather than trying to fight them with conventional weapons, to enlist the help of one of the greatest non-Jewish prophets of his time, Balaam. Balak hires Balaam to curse the Jewish people. Balaam attempts to fulfill his task from a number of lookout points, but in every place in which he tries to curse, God turns it into a blessing.

There are only a few *parashot* named after people. In three instances, we find *parashot* named after non-Jews: Noah, Jethro, and Balak. The first two, though, were important and respected figures: the Torah attests to the fact that Noah was perfectly righteous, and Jethro, Moses's father-in-law, comes to the desert after being moved by God's great miracles saving the Jewish people. He also merited having his suggestion to decentralize the judicial system accepted by Moses. Here, in *Parashat Balak*, we are dealing with an evil king who was interested in destroying the Jewish people, a kind of ancient Khamenei. It is reasonable to assume that the Jewish people rejected the man and his ways. Why, then, was he honored by having a *parasha* named after him?

Further study of the *parasha* reveals that in the end, Balaam, who wanted to curse the Jewish people, gave us blessings that have become national treasures. One of the most famous phrases that come from our *parasha* is: "How good are your tents, Jacob, your homes, Israel" (24:5). There is hardly a prayer book printed that does not open with that verse, and many synagogues are adorned with these words on their walls. Balaam expresses his wonder at the tents of Jacob and the dwellings of Israel. The Sages understood this as a reference to houses of study and synagogues, or to regular houses whose openings are oriented to maintain the personal modesty of their inhabitants. In another verse, Balaam says: "A star will shoot forth from Jacob, a scepter will arise from Israel" (24:17). These words became the motto of the Bar Kokhba rebellion, embodying the faith in Israel's revival after the long exile.

I always wondered why we needed a non-Jew, an outsider, to pay us these compliments and to say things that Jews did not find the courage to say. Do we need a stranger to tell us of what will happen in our houses of study over the course of our life as a nation? Are we unable to appreciate the wonderful spiritual creation of our own people, which developed even in difficult circumstances in North Africa and Europe? And regarding the star that went forth from Jacob, are we unable to see the unprecedented wonder of the revival of a nation from destruction after two thousand years on our own? Do we still need proof that our state actualizes the dreams of thousands of generations? Do we still need Balaam, or American Christians, to remind us of these miracles?

Perhaps someone involved in mundane difficulties is unable to raise their head and see all the good around them. Apparently, someone immersed in the house of study does not always appreciate what is happening on the national stage, and someone concerned with national developments is sometimes deaf to the wonderful notes emerging from the house of study. To accomplish this, we need someone to come from the outside, a stranger and even an enemy, to present us with a mirror with which to see ourselves. Balak was wicked, and wanted to hurt us, but through him, we learned to see ourselves from a wider perspective that was enlightening and eye opening.

Multiple solutions can be proposed to solve the issue of the *ḥaredi* community's integration into military service. At the root of the dispute lies a refusal of each group to recognize the value of the actions of the other. One side does not recognize the importance of "the dwelling places of Israel" and lacks respect for Torah study. The other side does not properly respect the State of Israel and its institutions, and therefore does not appreciate the importance of bearing its share of the burden of society. Only when we leave our own bubble and appreciate the general picture that Balaam presented, a picture of the glory of Torah and sovereignty, we will appreciate the importance of all of these forces, and be able to find a true, just solution to the problem.

Pinḥas

Who is Pinhas, and why did he merit having a *parasha* named after him? At the end of the previous *parasha,* the Torah recounted how the Jewish people engaged in licentious behavior with the daughters of Moab and Midian. God punishes the nation with a great plague that killed 24,000 people. Among those responsible for the severe actions that brought the plague were some of the tribal leaders. Pinḥas, Aaron the priest's grandson, took initiative and killed the prince of the tribe of Simeon, and as a result, the plague stopped.

Our *parasha* begins with God's words to Moses, telling him of the reward that Pinḥas will receive for his actions. God promises "an eternal covenant of priesthood" (25:13) to him and his children, and the crown jewel of his reward is: "My covenant of peace" (25:12). However, shortly thereafter, when Moses asks God to appoint his successor, God doesn't choose Pinḥas. Instead, He tells Moses: "Take Joshua son of Nun, a man infused with My spirit" (27:18). This seems to be a surprising appointment. True, we have already heard of Joshua as the "young disciple, who did not leave the tent" (Exodus 33:11). But does that mean that he is the right person to bear the burden of bringing the people into the Land of Israel? Wouldn't it have been preferable for someone with proven nerve and experience like Pinḥas to lead? It seems that the world of leadership is far more complicated than the world of the priesthood. Leadership needs much more than courage, nerve, and zealotry. Pinḥas was a man of many merits, but to lead the congregation, you also (and especially) need to know how to "walk in tandem with each person's spirit" (Rashi on Numbers 27:18). Rashi calls this capacity "tolerating each and every person according to their opinion" (ibid.). The zealous leader, by his nature, will see certain dimensions of reality in a magnified or exaggerated way. These disturb him, causing him to set out on a crusade against them whose end is unclear. Moreover, it is not always the case that the cause that he sees as the most significant for our future is actually the topic over which it is worth debating.

The responsible, mature leader, on the other hand, who wants to be a shepherd for the entire congregation, needs to enlist his leadership, intelligence, and power to form an opinion, a strategy, and tactics that consider the needs and dreams of the people as a whole. He then needs to approximate the best course of action when a decision is needed.

This would seem to be an impossible mission. How can someone "be tolerant of each person's opinion," when everyone says different and opposing things which demand fundamentally different reactions? It is sufficient to randomly sample from the debates that ignited public interest in the last decades in order to understand the difficulty. How should a leader act when he knows that there are forces in the country that oppose a law in all of its versions, while many others forcefully demand it? How should a leader act when he has a strongly secular population in his country alongside a strongly religious one? Are all models of neighborliness doomed to failure?

The answer lies in the phrase in God's words: "A man infused with My spirit." Does the leader act out of a spirit of dedication that animates him, or does he oscillate along with the spirit of the times? When a leader acts out of a profound, comprehensive spiritual vision, and also has the ability to listen to each person and tolerate them and their opinion, he will be admired even if he does things that are seen as opposed to the values of a particular sector in society. When a leader encounters his nation on the spiritual level, a path can be found in which dispute does not tear the nation to pieces, but rather contributes to the development and success of all parts of the nation.

Matot

One of the most interesting stories in our *parasha* is the encounter with the first people to emigrate from Israel, the first people who wanted to separate themselves from the community and to take care of their own interests. Sometimes people think that the existence of Jewish communities outside of Israel is solely the result of a historical error – the long exile responsible for the nation's residence outside the borders of their own land. This would seem to be a common misunderstanding. We might want to think that this is how Diaspora communities were created. However, a quick glance at the nation's history reveals that there were almost always parts of the people who lived outside of Israel, even when they had the opportunity to live within it in relative security.

In our *parasha*, the Torah recounts that the members of two tribes, Gad and Reuben, had many sheep. When they arrived in the land of Gilead, they identified a place with the optimal environmental conditions for raising their sheep. Therefore, they turned to Moses and the other leaders of the nation, and asked their permission to settle in that area, and not to cross the Jordan to the Promised Land with the rest of the nation. Moses's reaction was biting and harsh: "Will your brothers go out to war while you sit here?!... And here you are, a brood of sinners, taking your fathers' places" (32:6–14). In plain words, Moses identifies that the tribes want to avoid the burden of conquering the land. He expresses the concern that their behavior will cause the other tribes to lose heart, and to fear entering the land. This would be a repetition of the sin of the spies, as if forty years of wandering in the desert had not been enough for them, and they were willing to risk an additional punishment and an additional delay of their entrance into the land. In response to Moses's words, the leaders of the tribes declare that this was not their intention; they are willing to fully participate in the conquest of the land. Moses has them take a double oath to this effect, with a formula that leaves no room for misunderstanding. If they will lead the war efforts, they will be allowed to inherit the land of Gilead, and if they don't do so, they will not be allowed to inherit it. Their refusal to keep their promise will be considered a grave sin against God and against the people.

The commentators disagree about the nature of the original intention of the tribes of Gad and Reuben. Did Moses make a mistake in understanding their intentions, or did Moses's harsh words cause them to change their plan and accept full collaboration with the efforts to conquer the land? I always wondered about what really bothered Moses. Was it the desire to remain in an area blessed with rich pastures, with endless possibilities for economic development, over entering the Holy Land with endless ideals and spirituality, close to the Temple and Jerusalem? Or was it their disconnection from the people, and their placing the burden of waging war on other tribes?

A careful reading of the verses shows that Moses connects these two elements. Upon finishing his speech to the errant tribes, he uses a unique phrase: "You may return and be clear before the Lord and before Israel" (32:22). Moses understands that the problem with the tribes' behavior goes beyond the religious question of whether it is permissible for them to stay in the grazing land on the other side of the Jordan. He sees their behavior as a social failure, and wonders what the rest of the tribes will think about it. This is also part of what a person needs to consider when making a decision.

The individual and the leader have a double responsibility. He must be honest with himself, and with his own conscience and feel whole with God. But this alone is insufficient; there is also the social, public truth.

The responsibility to be honest and uncorrupt toward the people around us is also part of our Torah. Our Sages in the Talmud describe different restrictions placed on public officials in order to prevent rumors being spread about them. These were enacted based on the verse "You must be clear before the Lord and before Israel" that appears in our *parasha*. In the Grace After Meals, we say: "Let us find favor and good judgment in the eyes of God and of people"; our spiritual aspiration is for the commitment to these values to always guide our behavior. It is worthwhile to note the order: first "God" and then "man." A person's commitment to their absolute values comes before finding favor in society's eyes; but nevertheless, the latter still has an important place within the set of our considerations; we cannot simply ignore it.

Masei

Parashat Masei is the last *parasha* in the book of Numbers. The Jewish people are at the end of their wanderings in the desert, an exceedingly long journey that has lasted forty years, and now stand at the eastern border of the Promised Land. The scent of the imminent entry into the land wafts from every chapter of this section.

Thus, we have a review summarizing all of Israel's journeys in the desert, ending with God's command to enter the land and inherit it. Later, the Torah traces the borders of the land that the people are meant to conquer, gives us a list of the names of the people responsible for dividing up the land among the tribes, and establishes the boundaries of green spaces that will surround the cities. But one topic is surprising and seems out of place: the extensive discussion of the laws of intentional and unintentional murderers: "When you cross the Jordan into the land of Canaan, select towns to be your refuge cities, to which a person who kills another unintentionally may flee" (35:10–11).

Twenty-five verses are dedicated to the manner in which society is meant to deal with intentional murderers, as well as people who injure and kill out of negligence and inattention. The Torah warns against accepting a monetary ransom (presumably from rich families) as a substitute for the established punishment for an intentional murder, and ends with the harsh words: "The land can have no atonement for the blood that is shed in it – except through the blood of the one who shed it" (35:33).

The Torah has already explained the severity of the prohibition of murder on a number of occasions. It did so in *Parashat Noaḥ,* and included it in the Ten Commandments. Why discuss it again, and at such great length? In a moral society, there is no reason to explain why it is forbidden to murder. Why does the Torah see the need for this, particularly now, on the eve of the Jewish people's entry into the land?

It seems that the Torah is teaching us a critically important lesson in these verses. Entering the land will involve great wars, which automatically degrade the value of human life. Soldiers become habituated to difficult sights, and this can lead to a society in which the loss of life is not viewed with such severity, as we have already seen death with our own eyes time and time again. Precisely for this reason, the Torah comes to emphasize its warning about the value of human life. We are not pacifists or moral hypocrites who hurry to turn the other cheek to one who strikes them. But, at the same time, we are zealous about the spilling of innocent blood. This is true regarding car accidents, and it is meant to be true of life in general. There is no need to spend time speaking of the severity of an intentional murderer. People like that are usually a negligibly small minority within civilized society. But regarding negligence and accidental killing, a person would seem to have the excuse that "I didn't mean it, I made a mistake, I didn't estimate the distance accurately." Precisely because this claim is so human and understandable, we need to be prepared for it and to make sure that it doesn't erode our sense of the importance of human life. This claim is problematic not because mistakes aren't possible. We're all human, we all make mistakes. But someone who knows that he will have to stand before the bereft family who is suffering terribly because of his negligence will think twice about the way he drives. Someone who understands how miserable his own family will be on account of his dangerous behavior on the beach will act all the more carefully while swimming, and only in places that are safe and legal.

These portions are always read during the period called "*Bein HaMetzarim*," the days between Shiva Asar BeTamuz and Tisha BeAv. These are days that are prone to calamity, in two senses. On the one hand, all the greatest national tragedies throughout Jewish history took place during this time period. On the other hand, in recent generations, these days are the very heart of summer vacation, and are prone to tragedy in another way – personal tragedies that youngsters on vacation tend to bring on themselves. One young man, a friend of my son, a boy sweet as honey, told me of how he accidentally found himself in a dangerous situation: an unexpected climb on a cliff between heaven and earth, a hairsbreadth away from death. We often hear stories of hikers encountering such dangers because of activities which had not been planned out properly beforehand.

Someone trained by the end of the book of Numbers, who understands the tremendous value of human life (his own and that of all others) will always remember the responsibility to be cautious not to harm another person, whether on purpose or by accident.

POCKET

Deuteronomy

דברים

Devarim

The last book of the Pentateuch, and the name of the *parasha* that begins it, is *Devarim*. Literally, it means "words," named for Moses's speeches before his death in the plains of Moab, on Israel's eastern border. The entire book is true to this name, the majority of it being a summary of Moses's words to the nation in the month before his death. The book begins on the first day of the month of Shevat and ends on the seventh of Adar – thirty-seven days in total. When approaching the topic of Moses's words, we are automatically reminded that we are speaking of the same man who said, at the time of his appointment, "I am not a man of words; I was not yesterday, nor the day before...I am slow of speech and tongue" (Exodus 4:10). Now he is giving speeches that would make the greatest of rhetoricians proud. The difference between the man who needed his brother Aaron to be the mediator between himself and the nation (as God said, "and Aaron your brother will be your prophet"; Exodus 7:1) and the man who delivers inspiring oratories begs the question: What caused this marvelous transformation?

There are those who explain that initially, before his very first task as a leader, Moses was simply saying that he did not have the requisite skills to speak before kings and ministers to convince Pharaoh to let the Jewish people out of Egypt. He never thought that he would not be able to engage in a serious and significant discourse with the people. But this explanation does not fit the words that Moses himself uses: "For I am slow of speech and tongue." This does not sound simply like a difficulty managing diplomatic engagements. A look at the Midrash will offer us another explanation of the Sages.

> It is comparable to a merchant selling purple cloth. The king called to him and said: Do you have purple cloth? He said: No. The king responded: But I heard that you sell purple cloth! The merchant replied: Relative to you, my merchandise is insignificant. Thus did Moses tell God: Relative to You, I am not a man of words. (Deuteronomy Rabba 1:7)

When Moses speaks to the Jewish people, however, he is most certainly a gifted "man of words." According to this midrashic explanation, Moses's words were relative: compared to God, he is not a man of words. When he needs to stand before God or to compare himself to God, he is speechless. But he can certainly speak to the nation. The difficulty with this explanation is that no one asked Moses to describe his talents vis-à-vis God. His central task was to speak to the people and to Pharaoh. Of what relevance is his difficulty speaking before God?

Our Sages seek to teach us a fascinating lesson regarding leadership in general, and Moses's leadership in particular. The leader is meant to bring God's word to the people, and this Moses knew how to do well. But Moses understood his task to be far more than that. He would need to represent the people to God, and for this task he felt inadequate. Only one who understands the people, shares their pain, and represents them faithfully to God can be the loyal shepherd who also demands the people listen to God's words. After forty years of endless sacrifice on behalf of the Jewish people, despite all of their failures, Moses found that he had the moral legitimacy to reprimand them for their mistakes. A leader who was willing to say, "Erase me from the book that You have written" (Exodus 32:32) when he saw God ready to destroy the people after the sin of the Golden Calf, can also demand of the people to live up to the expectations God has of them, expectations which Moses himself did meet. This kind of leader will also enjoy the trust of the people, and can expect that his words will be heard and accepted.

The Midrash continues and suggests another explanation for the gap between Moses's speech difficulties in Exodus and his copious speech in our *parasha*: words of Torah have reparative power. Every person has limited abilities and talents. Moses was also limited in a number of areas, but the moment that he accepted the task, he enjoyed new energies. Moses called himself "slow of tongue and speech" before the nation accepted the Torah and their mission. After a person or a nation accepts a meaning and mission for their life, they are capable of handling their physical disabilities and overcoming them.

Va'etḥanan

Parashat Va'etḥanan, the second *parasha* in the book of Deuteronomy, begins with the heartrending personal story of Moses begging God to allow him to enter the land despite the sin of striking the rock at the waters of Meribah. God's response is "No," instructing Moses to ascend to the top of the mountain and to see Israel from there, "for you will not cross the Jordan" (3:27). Moses will only merit seeing the land from afar. He will never enter it.

I have always tried to imagine this figure of Moses, the greatest of leaders, yearning to bring his people into the Promised Land. God allows him a taste, letting him conquer lands on the eastern side of the Jordan, but not to reach the place he so desperately desired. What did he feel? Was he angry, sad, or frustrated? What does he do with all of those emotions? It is important to remember that Moses has many claims against the people, many of which he expresses in this *parasha*. Essentially, he says that the nation is to blame for the fact that God will not let him into the land: "The Lord was enraged with me because of you" (3:26). It is fascinating to see, particularly on this backdrop, what Moses does when his pleas and requests are not answered.

What would we have done in his place? Would we have a tantrum and say, "Well, if you don't want me, I will leave and worry about myself"? Or is there another way to react? The Torah relates that immediately after God's unequivocal answer, which clarified beyond any doubt that Moses will not enter the land, Moses reacted with a number of concrete actions. The central one was to deliver a series of speeches that surviewed the range of challenges that the people would face upon entering the land – religious, military, and economic. Moses could have said, "This is not my responsibility anymore, let them figure it out themselves." We all know managers or leaders who are not interested in training proper replacements, so that everyone will only remember their success.

Here we are witness to a man for whom the pain of the nation was his own personal pain, and who therefore does everything in order to benefit the people, even in his absence. He does not shy away from saying difficult things that people will have a hard time hearing. He warns of possible exile from the land, under certain conditions (as indeed happened; it is no coincidence that we read these words in the synagogue on Tisha BeAv). But these words come from a heart full of love and worry, not from anger or frustration. Even when Moses speaks of the most difficult times that our nation will face, he prophesies: "In your distress, when all these things have happened to you, in the days to come, you will finally return to the Lord your God" (4:30). The nation will never completely disconnect from its roots.

In this *parasha*, Moses teaches us how a leader whose dreams and aspirations were not realized ought to act. A leader who sees the nation as the central value understands that he needs to set his own needs and desires aside, and to ask what is truly good for the people. He must understand that his own place as leader is secondary to the success of his nation. We expect of ourselves and of our leaders that we will know how to set the good of the state before individual considerations, and this is our comfort from the difficulties that we face together while building the social and economic foundations of the State of Israel.

Ekev

Our Sages say that the word "*ekev*," literally, "heel," hints at things that a person treads upon with their heel. The greatest danger on a person's doorstep is not the big sins, rather the small infringements that we are used to violating from time to time frightened Moses more than anything else. When you dig down to the core of the *parasha*, you can understand what this means. In general, the Torah is involved with warnings about what may happen to the nation as a result of their encounter with the local economic, material culture in the Promised Land. We should remind ourselves what we're talking about: a nation that was enslaved for two hundred years, that never had an experience of economic comfort, a nation that for the last forty years had become accustomed to life in the desert, a place with no water or vegetation, a place in which they were completely dependent on God's grace to survive. While the manna descended next to their tent every day, they were never able to really rely on this.

To be honest, even if not everyone loved the manna, it did arrive regularly, without any work or effort attached. But on the other hand, there was no way to store excess manna, and anyone who did quickly saw how it became moldy and full of worms. Now that the nation readies itself to enter the land, they are about to face a culture shock. On the one hand, they will need to go to work: to thresh, plant, and wait for the rain to fall. Nothing is certain, and even God's hand will not be directly experienced as it was in the desert. There will be room for economic initiative and creativity. And the people will be allowed to accumulate wealth without worrying about worms in their wheat. In the desert, everyone ate the same food, without any difference between rich and poor, but in the Land of Israel, after only a few months there will be those who succeed and those who fail. The concern that bothers Moses is a natural one: How will the people deal with this change? What will the rich do? How will they treat their friends, who were not as lucky as they? I remember as a child when immigrants arrived to Israel from countries that did not enjoy the economic plenty of the West. They would enter the store and be astonished by all of the different types of cheeses arranged on the shelves.

But the most concerning of all is the sin of arrogance of those who succeeded. In the Torah's words: "Your heart may become proud, forgetting the Lord your God.... You might be tempted to say to yourself, 'My power, the strength of my own hand, have brought me this great wealth'" (8:14, 17). Financial success can cause one to forget their system of values, and is even more prone to estranging us from ourselves and from our identities as Jews and as human beings. We may suddenly find more in common with the wealthy members of Canaanite society than with our own nation and family. This is the greatest concern, and the Torah's only solution is memory: We must remember where we come from. The Torah commands us to remind ourselves that we were not born with a silver spoon in our mouths, and that, therefore, there is also no guarantee that it will remain there. A person who lives in this way knows that sometimes, he may need to tighten his belt more than he is used to, because success and plenty are not to be taken for granted.

There is something about the reality of our lives in a land in which we are in control of our fate that creates a built-in uncertainty. Will rain fall or not? Will taxes be raised or lowered? What will happen to the price of gas? We don't enjoy the certainty of the generation that ate manna in the desert. But through this lack of certainty, we become used to the idea that a person's life is more than his bread and water, but the content with which he fills his life. When we apply this philosophy to our lives, life in the land, with all of its material challenges, becomes something promising and hopeful. The life in the land is hard, but full of meaning. The life of the desert-dweller, living under the clouds of glory, is secure and certain, but it lacks the sense of renewal reserved for a person who lives in Israel.

Re'eh

Parashat Re'eh begins a series of four *parashot* that list, in great detail, a large number of mitzvot that the nation is commanded to follow upon their entrance into the Land of Israel. Some of these commandments were relevant in the desert as well, and were taught in previous books of the Torah. Their mention here serves as a reminder. Indeed, this is the nature of the book of Deuteronomy, whose Latin name echoes the Hebrew name "*Mishneh Torah*," a repetition of the law. Some of the mitzvot, however, are new. We hadn't heard them earlier, but now, when preparing to enter the land, it is time to receive them. One of the verses describing such a commandment says the following: "When the Lord your God has enlarged your territory as He has promised, and you say, 'I shall eat some meat,' because you have the urge to eat it, you may eat meat whenever you desire it" (12:20). To put it plainly, when we live in Israel, we will be permitted to eat meat whenever we want to. But this translation loses some of the original meaning, because the verse did not only mention the allowance to eat meat, but also placed it into a certain context and framework. The verse determined that this permission is somehow connected to the realization of "when the Lord your God has enlarged your territory." This condition is perplexing and seems irrelevant: How is the size of our territory connected to eating meat?

The simple explanation is that when we were in the desert, God commanded the Jewish people to bring all meat as a sacrifice in the Tent of Meeting, because of its geographic proximity. In Israel, on the other hand, where they may live much further away from the Temple, they are permitted to eat meat as they please.

But the verse did not simply say, "When you come to the land." Rather, it specifically mentioned "enlarging your territory," and thus hinted at what kind of expansion is needed to allow the consumption of meat. Rashi writes: "The Torah taught proper behavior, that a person should only desire meat from a state of plenty and wealth." What does this mean?

It is in a person's nature to desire things even without

any medical or biological need for them. Often, a person feels like they need whatever is common among their friends and neighbors, even if it isn't something they can really afford. As a result, a person will experience a sense of deficiency, even though, from an objective perspective, they have everything they really need. The Torah teaches proper behavior, that a person should only eat meat (a synonym in that time for luxury items) in a state of plenty. If you have enough – *bon appétit*! But if you don't, don't exert yourself to attain it. In other words, luxuries can be legitimate if you have the money to finance them, but a person should not constantly desire what he does not have.

This advice would seem particularly important for us in the age of plenty in which we live. A world overflowing with abundance can make us forget what is necessary and what is a luxury. We often forget that some things that we view as necessities (a better car, fancy vacations, advanced devices) are things that our parents could only dream of. The outcome is twofold: We enter a tailspin which, beyond the holes it creates in our savings, also implants a sense of bitterness and frustration that we cannot attain what our neighbors have. Hence, the importance of the Torah's instruction. During difficult times, when everyone is tightening their belts, it is easy to be happy with the little that we have. It is particularly during a period of abundance, when class differences become more acute, that it is important to cultivate a sense of satisfaction with what we have, rather than looking at what we don't. The Torah taught us proper behavior, only to eat meat in a state of plenty.

Shofetim

Parashat Shofetim primarily discusses the structures of governance in the future Israelite kingdom. The *parasha* opens with the establishment of a tribal judicial system in each city, above which is a supreme court to which all are subject. In parallel, the Torah instructs us to choose a king who will be responsible for national policy and the army. The Torah places strict limits on both of these frameworks, and warns those responsible for them against taking bribes, biased judgment, authoritarian governance, and haughtiness.

At the end of the *parasha* there is an unusual commandment regarding the case of a person found killed in the field whose killer is unknown. The Torah sets out a detailed procedure. The elders of the nearest city bring a calf that was never used for plowing or bearing a burden to a stream surrounded by unworked lands, and there they break the calf's neck. Some of the sages of the Sanhedrin attend the ceremony, and the elders must wash their hands before them and declare: "Our hands did not spill this blood, and our eyes did not see" (21:7).

Many wonder about the meaning of this ceremony and its many symbols. Why take a young calf, and why to a stream whose lands were never worked? What need is there to embarrass the elders and require them to declare that they were not involved in this sin? Does anyone really think they had anything to do with this murder? It is reasonable to assume that the ceremony uses a young calf that never worked, in a desolate place, to symbolize the great tragedy of a person who lost his life before having an opportunity to raise a family and see his progeny. But we still need to understand the statement of the elders.

The talmudic sources suggest two possibilities. In the Babylonian Talmud, our Sages explain that the leaders of the city want to establish that they did not send the victim from the city without providing appropriate escort or provisions, and therefore, that they are not responsible, even indirectly, for what happened. In modern terms, the elders needed to declare that there was appropriate lighting on the roads, that the traffic lights were working, that the police and security forces acted responsibly, and that people could feel safe. This explanation focuses on the role of leadership to ensure the personal safety of the victim. In the Jerusalem Talmud, written in Israel, a much more far-reaching explanation is offered, according to which the elders need to declare that they didn't send the *murderer* without proper escort or provisions. Obviously, the identity of the murderer is unknown, and therefore, the significance of this declaration is that they provided proper provisions and escort to every person who passed through their town. This raises the level of responsibility significantly. The authorities are essentially committing to the fact that they made sure that there would not be anyone hungry enough that it led them to hurt someone.

If we combine these two explanations, the elders are declaring that they protected all travelers from violence by ensuring that no one could be injured by someone else, and that no one would feel the need to do so. This declaration may also be seen as including the promise that the justice system was not overly forgiving in previous cases of violence. All of this is part of the commitment of the elders to their townspeople, and to God. It would seem that to be able to make such a declaration, they need to carry with them a profound faith in the quality of their leadership. And it would seem that the Sages are teaching us something important about the meaning of violence in their time, and perhaps in our time as well.

It all begins with how we escort and accompany the murderers, that is, the entire population that might potentially hurt someone else. In other words – all of us. This accompaniment involves the entire justice system, to teach us just how severe these matters are. Even more importantly, it demands activating the educational system to teach self-control and respect for one another and for property. If we project zero tolerance for all types of violence to our students, they will understand that this is a line that can never be crossed. The more we, as adults, will be determined to pass on the message of the importance of every human life, the more we will have the right to say that our hands did not spill blood in Jerusalem or in Netanya.

Ki Tetzeh

Parashat Ki Tetzeh is one of the most eclectic *parashot* in the Torah. There is almost no realm of Jewish law that it doesn't mention. Interpersonal laws and religious laws, civil laws, personal status, and criminal law. Laws related to the family are especially prominent, such as the laws of marriage, the possibility of divorce, and more.

One of the more remarkable laws in the *parasha* is called the law of the rebellious son. Here's how it goes: A child in his early teenage years (around the age of bar mitzva) causes problems at home. In the language of Scripture: "He doesn't listen to the voice of his father or mother" (21:18). They hit him, but it doesn't help. Things get worse, the child steals wine and meat (or cans of beer, or bottles of tequila, the keys to the car, etc.), the parents warn him, but the child continues behaving improperly. At this point, the parents give up, turn to the court, and declare for all to hear: We give up, this son of ours is a glutton and a drunkard, he doesn't do anything, and just embarrasses us. The elders of the congregation instruct the people of the city to stone the young man and kill him.

It's a very strange law. While the death penalty does feature in Jewish tradition, it is usually for the most severe violations, like murder and idol worship, not for theft. Moreover, we are speaking of a minor, and yet we're giving him the death penalty. Our Sages dealt with these difficulties, explaining that the Torah foresaw the end of this child, and understood that someone who is capable of stealing from his parents today will one day steal from other people, and will ultimately end up killing someone. Therefore, better to stop the criminal while he is still young. In other words, the halakha is suggesting a preventative measure – killing a young man, before he deteriorates to committing severe actions with which society will have a hard time coping. But even this answer is far from satisfying, as we know that in general, a person is only judged for things that he has already done, not for things that he may do in the future. This would seem to be one of the reasons that the Rabbis said that the law of the rebellious son was never applied, and never will be, and the whole topic was only written in order to interpret it and receive reward. In other words, they are saying that the Torah wanted to teach educational principles by way of this story, not practical advice meant to be carried out.

What, then, are the ideas that we can learn from this sad story of a young man who has gone in a bad direction? It would seem that the most important question in this story is: What caused this? The Torah does not state this explicitly, but there are commentaries that try to extrapolate the roots of the problem from the language that the Torah uses to formulate the story.

The Torah relates the essence of the story in this way: This young man's problem is that "he does not listen to his father's voice or his mother's voice." The word "*kol*," "voice," appears twice. Why didn't the Torah simply say: "He does not listen to his parents' voice"? Could it be that the seeds of this tragedy were planted by the parents speaking in two different, perhaps opposing, voices? We all understand that in a family in which the father educates exclusively toward achievement, while the mother emphasizes ethical values, or vice versa, the child will be confused when he tries to establish his values and priorities.

If we look even more broadly, and pay attention to the

wide variety of voices that our children hear – is this not a recipe for confusion? If the parents' voice is in conflict with the voice of the school, and these are both different than the voice of contemporary culture and media, then we have a surefire recipe for getting educationally lost. Rabbi Auerbach, of blessed memory, once explained to a father who asked him why his son had gone off on the wrong path, that it was based on the way the father had denigrated the son's teachers. The son wasn't able to resolve the contradiction; on the one hand, to hear derision, and on the other hand to listen and be educated. The story of the rebellious son confronts us with the need to create a clear educational vision that unites all of those things that influence our children's value system.

Ki Tavo

There isn't usually any correlation between the *parasha* being read in the synagogue and the calendar, since the reading continues according to *parasha,* from Genesis (after Simḥat Torah) until the end of Deuteronomy at Simḥat Torah of the following year. The exception is our *parasha, Ki Tavo.* The Talmud relates that as far back as the time of Ezra (at the beginning of the Second Temple era), the Sages established that this *parasha* would always be read before Rosh HaShana. Why so? So that "the year and its curses will end" (and we are accustomed to add: "And the new year and its blessings will begin").

Why did they do this?

In two places in the Torah, we find verses that are referred to as "verses of rebuke." In its chapters of rebuke, the Torah warns the people what will happen if we don't follow it, and describes the plentiful wealth and abundance that we will merit if we do follow the Torah's laws. The expressions used in these verses are exceedingly harsh. The following is only a sampling of the Torah's curses in *Parashat Ki Tavo*: "Cursed shall you be in the town and cursed shall you be in the field…. The Lord will send upon you curse…until you are destroyed…. The Lord will afflict you with consumption, fever, inflammation…. You will be incessantly abused and crushed" (28:16–33), etc., etc. These are difficult things to say or to read, nor is it easy to hear them. This is presumably the reason for the custom to read this section in a low voice. We want to suppress and deny them as much as possible. There are communities in which the custom is to let the beadle or the Torah reader read the verses of the rebuke, since the rest of the congregants are reluctant to do so, fearing that this would bring an evil eye upon them. But fear is not the main problem: these things can cause a kind of paralysis, and scare people off from engagement in the Jewish people and its covenant with God.

I always wondered why these verses are read before Rosh HaShana and not after it. Why was it so important to the Sages that the curses remain a part of the previous year, and not enter into our new year? Wouldn't it be better to read these verses so that we more fully appreciate the severity of the personal, family, and communal questions that face us, and weigh them with appropriate seriousness? Wouldn't we want ourselves, or our leaders, to read the *parasha* of rebuke before making an important decision?

The answer, apparently, is no. It is impossible to move forward with life (in all areas) if we are always concerned about possible curses. A person is meant to tread carefully and to use his best judgment in order to come to a decision, but he also needs to believe in himself and in his capacity to make decisions. When the Sages said, "Let the year and its curses end" (Megilla 31b), they wanted to increase our belief in ourselves, and in our ability to choose properly. They didn't want us to lose our faith in our most precious human ability: to improve and change. Rashi relates, following the *Midrash Tanḥuma,* that after hearing all the curses, the nation blanched and said, "Who can live up to all of this?" At that point, Moses called to them and started reassuring them: "You've made God angry many times, and He hasn't destroyed you" (Rashi on Deuteronomy 29:12). Why did Moses say this? He loses all of the deterrent power of the rebuke! But it seems that Moses understood that fear can also paralyze. The consequences of straying from the path will be severe. They sound terrible, they are truly frightful, but we have survived until now, and we will continue to do so, if only we know how to take the curses into account, while also knowing how to leave them in the previous year and move forward, fearlessly.

Nitzavim

Parashat Nitzavim speaks of the covenant that God makes with the Jewish people on the eve of their entry into the Land of Israel. It opens with these words: "All of you are standing today before the Lord your God – the leaders among you, the tribes, the elders and officials, all the men of Israel…from woodcutter to water drawer – to enter into the covenant of the Lord your God" (29:9–11). The Torah has many ways in which it describes the Jewish people: community, congregation, nation, and more. But our *parasha* is the only place in the Torah in which all of the strata of society are mentioned in detail, and this demands an explanation. What makes this covenant even more unique is the fact that it is made not only with the current generation, but with all future generations throughout Jewish history. This caused commentators to ask how one generation can make a commitment in the name of its children who were not asked and did not give their consent. Later, the Torah relates to the possibility that there will be those in the future who seek to abandon the covenant, believing it possible to release themselves from the commitment to this historic agreement between the people and their God. The Torah warns against this line of thinking, citing its dangerous ramifications. Why not allow a person who does not feel connected to go on their own way, just as many Jews indeed did throughout history, deciding to "graze in foreign fields"?

The simple explanation is that the agreement is made with the nation as a whole, and therefore, it obligates the whole. So that everyone will feel they are bound by this agreement, they all need to be present at the time of its signing, and therefore, all of those present at this event are mentioned in detail. According to this logic, we would have to say that the act of the parents obligated their future progeny, and therefore, the presence of all the strata of the people at this covenant created the obligation on their children in future generations.

But our Sages imbued these verses with an additional dimension. God does not only choose the righteous and the leaders to constitute His nation. He is interested in an entire people. The Jewish people was not created only to cultivate Nobel Prize winners, even though we are particularly proud of them. Nor was it created to cultivate outstanding athletes (even if they would bring us more medals). We are in favor of excellence, but our destiny as a people is actually to emphasize that we seek as a whole, in all sectors of society, to be good and ethical in the eyes of God and man. If one part of the people doesn't take part in the covenant, we lose our ability to realize our purpose – to create a wholesome, healthy society. As individuals, we can survive without others, but we can no longer represent the nation as a whole. Therefore, the Torah emphasizes that we all stood at the making of the covenant, from the woodcutters to the drawers of water. Without them, we are not the same nation.

There are those who explained that the verse "You stand today" hints at Rosh HaShana, when the nation stands before God in judgment. We can suggest, then, that our ability to stand before God in prayer, so He will decree a good year upon us, depends on the understanding that we can only come before Him all together, as a whole nation.

For years, there have been many dangers that we have consistently faced, and other dangers arise anew, that do not distinguish between those on the front and those at home, between rich and poor or religious and secular. We must strengthen the covenantal bonds among ourselves so that we will be capable of standing before God to ask for His help in the conflict between ourselves and our neighbors.

Vayelekh

Parashat Vayelekh focuses on Moses's last days before leaving this world. And lo, after an entire book dedicated to Moses's warnings to the nation regarding what will happen if they don't follow the right path, God tells him: "Soon, you are going to rest with your ancestors. And this people will begin to stray after the foreign gods of the land into which they are going" (31:16). Basically, God is telling Moses: Don't think that your words have penetrated their hearts and have actually done something. They will fail, and I will be angry with them, hide My face from them, and many calamities will befall them, until the point that "on that day they will ask, 'Have not these troubles come upon us because our God is not in our midst?'" (31:17). Moses then gathers the people and declares that he, too, knows that after his death they will corrupt their ways and anger God with their actions.

There is no way to react to these verses other than depression. If the results of this game are all known from the start, what is the point of playing? Why even try? After all, Moses, and even God, are saying that they know that we will sin and fall. What, then, is the point of trying to act Jewish and to maintain this identity, if we know from the get-go that our chances of success are slim to none?

Indeed, some people will read these verses and tell themselves that there is no point in making an effort, since everything in this world is corrupt and rotten in any case. In situations of crisis and trials, everyone fails; there is no point in being good in an evil world.

But it is possible to read these verses from the exact opposite perspective, and this is the one that is worthy of special attention. The Torah is telling us that it was given to us in an imperfect world, within a reality in which failure is common. We should not think that the One who gave us the Torah thought that we would live in the world of angels. On the contrary, He knew that most people would fail at different stages in their life. But nevertheless, every person, in spite of their occasional failures, would say that they want to live in a world of positive values, in a society in which goodness and justice rule. Moses's announcement of our impending failure is meant to encourage us. Its purpose is to tell us that despite the failures that certainly await us, we should not despair. An old hasidic saying suggests that man's greatest sin is the statement that God is not within him, meaning that he has lost his connection to the world of positive values within himself. Our purpose is to increase the recognition that there is no person for whom the good is not part of their awareness and their world view. At times it is concealed to others or to the person himself, but deep in his soul, every person yearns for a world of repair and increasing goodness. May we merit to see this good within ourselves and to empower it.

Haazinu

Many people call this *parasha* "the song of *Haazinu*," for three reasons. Firstly, the Torah refers to these verses as a "song," in God's words to Moses in the previous *parasha*: "So now write down this song and teach it to the Israelites" (31:19). The second reason relates to the way the verses appear – they are written in the Torah scroll in the form of a song, as short, metered lines of poetry, rather than prose. The third, and main reason, has to do with their content. These verses do not contain a historical event or words of rebuke for the future, but rather a description of the past, present, and future in poetic language. The purpose of this song is to be a living testimony for the nation of its past, of the good that God had done for them, and of what is in store for them if they stray from the proper path. These prophetic words were unfortunately fulfilled in their full severity. But the song also contains hope for the future, its verses foreseeing the nation's redemption in the end of days.

One of the verses that catches the eye with its relevance for our times is: "Remember the days of old, consider the years of ages past; ask your father, and he will tell you; your elders, and they will speak" (32:7). Moses seems, at first glance, to be calling for the study of history to be established as a required course in high schools and universities. And not only the history of the Jewish people is included, but the history of the entire world: "Remember the days of the world (in Hebrew, '*olam,*' 'of the world')."

What is the purpose of this study? The verse mentions the need to remember, and also to understand: "Consider the years of ages past." But the skeptic will rightfully ask: Does history really ever repeat itself in precisely the same way? Is it not pathetic to try to prepare for the wars of the future by studying the battles of the past? After all, there are significant gaps, technological and otherwise, between armies and cultures. How can studying the past help us?

We can understand the importance of historical memory and understanding in several ways. One can try to learn lessons from the behavior of nations in circumstances of stress or tranquility, and to extrapolate guidelines for best practices for mankind in similar circumstances. It is reasonable to assume that there is what to be gained from this study, but we cannot use these insights to predict what the future will bring, and therefore, these conclusions will have, by nature, limited usefulness. It would seem, rather, that the primary importance of learning and studying the past is its contribution to our recognition of the ways in which the actions of our predecessors influenced and formed our human and Jewish identity. In other words, many people might ask themselves the question: "What do I learn from the Holocaust?" Each person might come to different, and even opposite, conclusions from this study. There will be those who conclude that we can only rely on our own military power, while others will say that we should spread the nation out over the four corners of the earth, etc. One's conclusions will generally be a reflection of one's own preexisting opinions and beliefs. Historical facts generally serve to strengthen our existing assumptions.

But there is one thing that can't be disputed: It is clear that the Holocaust has a deep influence on us today. It is impossible to understand the public debate around the question of Iran without appreciating the influence of the

Holocaust on the nature of the discourse. Without knowing anything about the nature or likelihood of the threat, everyone understands that a nation that has suffered countless attempts to destroy it throughout history, from its exile in Egypt until the last Holocaust, has a survival instinct embedded deep in its DNA, along with a mechanism to warn it of impending danger.

It is reasonable to assume that a leader with a sense of history will act differently than a leader without a historical consciousness. We all pray that our leaders will "remember the days of old and consider the years of ages past," and will know how to make the right decisions for our future in this land.

Vezot Haberakha

It is interesting to consider how the Giver of the Torah chose to end His book:

> There has never arisen a prophet in Israel like Moses, whom the Lord knew face-to-face, in all the signs and wonders the Lord sent him to perform in Egypt, against Pharaoh, all his officials, and all of his land, and all the acts of a mighty hand and of terrifying power that Moses performed before the eyes of all Israel. (34:10–12)

The end of the book focuses on Moses's greatness in three areas. First, as a prophet: Moses was a prophet unlike any other who ever was or ever will be. This statement, it seems, is meant to caution and prepare the Jewish people for the challenges that will arise throughout their history, when they will need to face false prophets that arise from within and from outside the Jewish people.

The second area is the significance of the events in which Moses participated. The verse emphasizes that this is a man who was involved in the greatest miracles in human history. These are not merely nice folktales, but events responsible for dramatic changes in the history of nations; some of the miracles were performed before the eyes of the entire nation, and other nations were also involved in what transpired.

The third area requires some explanation. What is the meaning of the "terrifying power that Moses performed before the eyes of all Israel"? Does this hint at a reign of terror, God forbid, or to some specific event? If so, what is it? The Sages explain that this refers to when "Moses decided to break the tablets before their eyes, as it says: 'And I smashed them before you' (9:17), and God agreed to his decision, as it says: 'That (*asher*) you broke' (10:2) – good for you (*yishar koḥakha*) that you broke them" (Rashi on Deuteronomy 34:12, based on Tractate Shabbat 87a). In other words, the Torah is reminding us of the episode when Moses smashed the tablets of the covenant that God gave him, following the sin of the Golden Calf.

This is very unusual. Out of the forty years of Moses's leadership, Scripture chooses to emphasize the smashing of the tablets as the event mentioned at the conclusion of the Torah?! What is so unique about this event, and what is its significance specifically at the Torah's conclusion?

It would seem that our Sages wanted to express a profound idea regarding the understanding of the very essence of the Torah, and the difference between its study and other subject matters. When we finish reading the Torah, we have to ask ourselves: What have we gained from this study? Was this merely another nice book that caused us to think and which temporarily moved us, but which we immediately set aside to return to our usual ways, without it having left a lasting impression or having changed us in fundamental ways?

The Torah comes to remind us that at the beginning of the shared journey of the people of Israel with their Torah, a formative event took place that was meant to establish the relationship between ourselves and the Torah for the future. A mere forty days after the Torah was given, when the entire nation declared, "We will do and we will listen," accepting the prohibition against idol worship and bowing to a graven image, the nation did just that, bowing to the Golden Calf.

Moses's immediate, extreme response was: If so, there is no Torah. The Torah can't be something that sits on the shelf and doesn't change us. If it sits in the corner without affecting our consciousness in a deep way, it is better that it not be at all.

As the Torah comes to a close, a person must ask themselves the fundamental questions, in whose absence Torah study loses all meaning. Not only what did I learn from the Torah, but also (and primarily) what has the Torah taught me, how has it changed me, and what has it built within me.

POCKET

Special Parashot

פרשות מיוחדות

Shabbat Shuva

There are only a few Shabbatot named after the *haftara* that we read on them, and for good reason. The custom of reading the Torah is an earlier one; there are those who claim that the reading of the *haftara* was only established in reaction to Roman decrees that forbade reading the Torah, and that after the custom to read a chapter from the prophets that connects to the *parasha* became widespread, it was not canceled even after those decrees were canceled. In any case, it is certain that the custom of reading the *haftara* came later than the reading of the Torah. The Torah, dictated to Moses by God, is considered holier than the books of the prophets, and therefore it is logical that Shabbat should bear the name of the Torah portions read on them, and not the name of the *haftara*, which is of lesser importance.

But despite all this, there are a number of Shabbatot whose *haftara* overshadows even the *parasha* itself. Regardless of which *parasha* is read on the Shabbat between Rosh HaShana and Yom Kippur, the chapter from the prophets that we read will always be Hosea chapter 14. The chapter opens with the words "O Israel, return, go back to the Lord your God, for you have stumbled in your own sinfulness" (14:2), and the connection to the time of year we are in is clear: These are the ten days of repentance, which tradition heeds us to spend contemplating our behavior and trying to improve it. It could even be that this Shabbat's real name is "*Shabbat Teshuva*," named for the days of repentance of which it is a part.

But the question we need to ask is why the Sages established that we should read this chapter in particular. The books of the prophets are replete with chapters calling on the Jewish people to improve their behavior. What makes the prophecy before us from the book of Hosea uniquely appropriate for the days of repentance? It seems that this prophecy contains some symbols that connect it in a profound way to the historic consciousness of every Jew. Hosea was a member of the tribe of Reuben, whose founder, according to tradition, spent many days in fasting and sackcloth on account of his sin with his father's concubine, Bilha. He may be the first Jew who ever sinned and repented. He showed our people that there is a path to repentance, and as we will see further on, this is not something to be taken for granted. Our Sages said the following: "The Holy One, Blessed be He, said to Reuben: You were the first to begin with repentance; I swear by your life that Hosea, son of Beeri, your son, will open the way of repentance of Israel, as it says (Hosea 14:2): 'O Israel, return, go back to the Lord your God'" (*Pesikta Rabbati*, Ish Shalom edition, addendum 1, paragraph 3).

The central story in Hosea's prophecy also echoes the classic Jewish narrative. God commands Hosea to take a prostitute as a wife, and she gives birth to two children of unknown paternity. The prophet is asked to divorce his disloyal wife, but he has trouble doing so, because of his love for her. God uses this to explain to Hosea the depth of the connection between God and His people, a connection that makes it difficult for Him to separate Himself from them despite their frequent betrayals. The Midrash offers the following fascinating description:

> Hosea son of Beeri began to cry. The Holy One, Blessed be He, asked him: Hosea, why do you cry? He

> said: Because I had mercy on my wife and children. The Holy One, Blessed be He said to him: If you had mercy on your wife who is a prostitute and your children who are bastards, shall I not have mercy on My children, the children of My beloved Abraham, Isaac, and Jacob? For one who loves another must love their children. Immediately, Hosea awoke from his vision and began to praise Israel and said: "The children of Israel will number like the sands of the sea" (Hosea 2:1), and for this reason he said: "O Israel return, go back to the Lord your God, for you have stumbled in your own sinfulness" (Hosea 14:2). (Midrash Aggada, Buber edition, Leviticus 16)

Hosea was chosen because he was a prophet who personally experienced the nature of the connection between God and His people, and he is the one who is able to convey the faith that God has in us despite our frustrating failures and mistakes.

But the prophecy before us also has an additional dimension, expressed in the words "Take words of remorse with you" and "Instead of calves we offer You our words of prayer" (14:3). A sinner can often think that the process of repentance will demand intolerable physical or spiritual sacrifices. A person's evil inclination prevents him from beginning the process of repair by warning him that he will need to concede things that make up his very identity. He will need to sacrifice his life as he knows it, and this is something so difficult that he won't succeed. The prophet seeks to offer an alternative view by saying: "Take words of remorse with you." Speak with yourselves and with God, discuss what needs repair in your own words – this is the sacrifice that is demanded of you. Not to give up on your personality or altruistic self-sacrifice. Just words. With this sentiment, our *haftara* became the foundation of the Jewish world of repentance, the recognition of the need to verbally confess what needs improvement and repair, without the need for physical or spiritual suffering.

Parashat Shekalim

Our Sages established the reading of four special Torah readings during the month of Adar that are added to the normal reading, related to the upcoming holidays of Purim and Passover. The first Shabbat of these four is *Parashat Shekalim*. What is this portion about? And why do we read it specifically now?

The plain meaning of the verses does not hint at any connection to Purim or Passover. The portion discusses a law that establishes that when we want to count the nation for whatever purpose (taxes, war, or the like), this is done by collecting a half-shekel from each person included in the census. We should note that we are not talking about a contemporary half-shekel. The value of the Scriptural shekel is measured based on the value of silver, and can reach a cost of tens of modern Israeli shekels. The money collected from the census was used to purchase various public sacrifices in the Temple. The date chosen to renew the donation was the first of the month of Nisan, but the courts announce the need to donate the money a month before, around the first of Adar. Although, since the destruction of the Temple, we are no longer obligated to donate a half-shekel and this mitzva is no longer practiced, we read this portion on the Shabbat preceding the first of Adar as a reminder. This is the technical reason for this reading, but this explanation raises a number of questions. There are more commandments which no longer apply in our day, but we do not find that the Sages established a Torah reading in place of a command that we can no longer fulfill. For example, the Paschal sacrifice is no longer offered, but there is no custom to read the portion of the Paschal sacrifice on the fourteenth of Nisan or the Shabbat before it. Why did the Rabbis want to specifically increase our consciousness of the command of the half-shekel?

There happens to be another dimension to the connection between the portion of *Shekalim* and the current season. It is read two weeks before Purim. It is well known that Haman told Ahasuerus that he would collect ten thousand silver shekels on his behalf, in exchange for the permission to attack the Jewish members of the Persian empire. He thus sought to make up for the loss of income to the empire, it seems. The Talmud says about this: "It was known to the Holy One, blessed be He, that in the future, Haman would take shekels in exchange for Israel. Therefore, He preempted Haman's shekels with the shekels of the Jewish people" (*Midrash HaGadol,* Megilla 13). The midrash connects two events that would seem to have nothing to do with each other. God knows that Haman will want to give money to Ahasuerus, and therefore He preemptively told us to give shekels to our own King. What lies behind this midrash? Is this some kind of competition to see who gives money to the kingdom first?

The giving of the half-shekel, although it is a kind of a tax for the Temple, does not depend on a person's income. Everyone gives the exact same amount. This is not because God refrains from asking for greater generosity from the rich – when the Torah wants to ask the rich to open their pocketbooks, it does so without hesitation. But here the Torah asks for the opposite. The Torah wants us to understand that fundamentally, we are all equal, and public sacrifices will belong equally to the rich and to the poor. Moreover, we are told to give a half-shekel in order to instill in us the sense that we are each only a part of a whole. We need each other, and no one can rely only on themselves, even if they are exceedingly strong or wealthy. Haman saw a fractured, scattered people and said to Ahasuerus: If what you want is money, I can provide it for you. And the Jewish nation responds from the depth of its consciousness that although it often seems that we share no common denominator, we all still belong to a single inner point that connects us with our past and our future. When each person gives a half-shekel, or reads about this mitzva in the Torah, he remembers that the idea that we are all a part of a whole, the conception that we are one nation, is what caused the destruction of our enemies in those days at this time.

Parashat Zakhor

Parashat Zakhor is a small portion of only a few verses that appears in the book of Deuteronomy, toward the end of Moses's great speech before leaving this world. The portion commands us to "remember what Amalek did to you," and then continues to describe Amalek's actions: "He attacked you on the way, when you were tired and exhausted, striking down all the stragglers in your rear." The resounding final note of the portion is: "Blot out the memory of Amalek from beneath the sky. Do not forget" (Deuteronomy 25:17–19). Our Sages understood this as a command to read these verses in public once a year, because otherwise they will be forgotten. This is the only time that the Torah commands the nation to read from the Torah, and thus, even many women who don't generally attend, come to synagogue to hear it.

I always wondered why it's so important for us to remember the past. Why is it so important to remember that there was once a nation called Amalek that wanted to destroy us as we left Egypt? In our modern, global world where everyone is friends (at least on Facebook) isn't it more appropriate to educate the next generation of the rosy, happy future that awaits us if we would but be wise enough to develop the right education and the right technologies? Why not adopt the approach of Israel's former president Shimon Peres, to whom the following aphorism is attributed: "It is not important to study the history of the past. What is important is to focus on the achievements of the future"? Isn't it outdated to focus on the past? Logic dictates that we remember our past enemies in order to protect us from future attacks from those same enemies. But it has been thousands of years since we have been able to identify Amalek. What is the purpose of remembering someone if you don't have any idea of who he is or where, or whether, he exists?

It seems that people in general, and perhaps the Jewish people in particular, have a wonderful trait that seeks to believe that people are good, and that ignores the warning signals that enemies broadcast. Animals have senses that warn them of impending danger, causing them to automatically flee or protect themselves. But with people, even after we see all of the warning signs, we still need to evaluate and interpret our enemies' intentions. Even when a reliable intelligence agent from within Egypt passed along precise information about Egypt's battle plans on the eve of the Yom Kippur War, we can evaluate the situation and decide that there is a low probability of danger. When speaking of evaluations, there is ample space for interpretation, which at times is influenced heavily by ideology. The Jews of Europe were (for the most part) unable to believe that an enlightened nation like Germany, cradle of the new civilization, could have an army full of sadistic brutes. Could it be that in a place that plays Mozart and Beethoven, they will smash babies into the wall?! Could it be that in a place with over half a million members of clubs against cruelty to animals, they could force Jews into gas chambers, something they would never do to dogs?!

Apparently, it could indeed be. And one who doesn't remember this doesn't understand the complexity of the human race. Humans can be full of mercy and gentleness, but at the very same time also sink to the depths of cruelty: "Striking down all the stragglers in your rear." The enemy doesn't seek to fight with our very best soldiers. He seeks an easy target, the weakest points. The central tool that a person was given that allows him to analyze signs that present themselves to him is memory. Remembering Amalek is not about remembering a particular nation. It is first and foremost about remembering the evil embedded in humanity in general, and in the enemies of Israel in particular.

In these days that the Iranian enemy threatens our right to exist, the message of the obligation to remember feels more relevant than ever. Don't be fooled by those who say: "It can't be," "They don't really mean it seriously," "The world won't let it happen" (like it doesn't let the Syrians slaughter their own countrymen). Anything can happen.

Parashat Zakhor is always read on the Shabbat before Purim, because according to tradition, Haman was a descendant of Amalek. Amidst all the celebrations at the salvation of the Jewish people, we might forget that when you drink, you can't drive; that is, when we are drunk with happiness, we cannot rely on our memories and on our clear-headedness, and it is advisable to refrain from making decisions that call for good judgment and memory. Therefore, before we get drunk and dress up, it is a good idea to focus on some historical memory, so that the day after Purim, we will be ready to deal with the next Amalekite.

Parashat Para

The third *parasha* in the set of four special portions read during the month of Adar is called *Parashat Para,* which discusses the laws of purity of people who were defiled by coming into contact with the dead. According to the Torah, one who was defiled by the dead can only enter the Temple after a process of purification. The defilement lasts for seven days, during which time he must be sprinkled twice with water mixed with the ashes of the red heifer that was slaughtered and burned for that purpose. Why is this read now?

The previous two portions were mostly connected to Purim; the second two portions, *Parashat Para* and *Parashat HaḤodesh,* are connected to the approaching holiday of Passover. Jewish law states that a person who touches a dead body becomes ritually defiled, and therefore is unable to eat the Paschal sacrifice. Since Passover is approaching, we want anyone who became ritually impure to remember that soon, they need to come to Jerusalem to eat the Paschal sacrifice, and therefore they should be sure to purify themselves quickly. Generally, the average person in a city or village can be impure for an extended period of time (unless he is a priest, who is obligated to eat the donation to the priests in a state of purity), but during these days, when Passover approaches, we need to remind everyone who is impure, who may even have forgotten of their state of impurity, that they ought to purify themselves before ascending to Jerusalem. The Sages ascribed great importance to this reminder, with many seeing it as a biblical commandment, and not merely an enactment of the Rabbis. This opinion had practical significance, as men and women who did not always come to synagogue were careful to come on this Shabbat to hear the reading of *Parashat Para*.

Today, the Temple no longer stands, and so a simple question arises: What is the value of this reading in our time? We are not able to become purified, and it doesn't seem likely that the Temple will be built between Purim and Passover. Is this just a reading that conserves something from the past, or can we ascribe another layer of meaning to it? We can always claim, and rightfully so, that we are preparing ourselves for the day when these readings will be relevant and practical, and that such a reading maintains a certain consciousness and creates a sense of longing, but will this idea suffice to quench our thirst for a lesson from this portion?

Firstly, it is difficult to know how many people this reading was ever relevant for – how many people became impure because of contact with the dead in a given year. Logic would suggest that there were not very many. In any case, if we say that this reading was established by the Rabbis, it would seem that it was not read during the time that the Temple stood. Those who established this reading did so after the destruction of the Temple, when there was no longer any need to be purified. Why was this done? And even if we say that they did read this portion when the Temple stood, where do we find that we read from the Torah in order to remind the people to fulfill a commandment? Do we read a portion from *Parashat Aḥarei Mot* during the month before Yom Kippur to remind people that the holiest day is coming and they should begin repenting?

The reading of the Torah is the central tool with which the Sages teach us what topic should be at the center of the Jewish people's agenda at this time. What they are telling us through the reading of *Parashat Para* is that to be free, one must go through a process of purification. There can be no redemption without internal purification that precedes it, because without it, freedom will end in disaster. Achieving liberty is not merely a technical act of being freed from subjugation to a state of independence. Every subjugated person must ask himself what will guarantee that he himself does not become a subjugator. Is all we have done is to switch roles, or have we learned how people should truly act? The encounter of the subjugated with the subjugator often involves struggles and wars, conflicts and subterfuge, and at times even human casualties. A person can become inured to all these, and develop a haughty, insensitive way of thinking that denigrates human suffering when it is the suffering of one's opponent, and that ignores the usual rules of common courtesy between people. In order to cope with this, we need purification. We need to know that the contact with death is defiling, even when it is necessary. The encounter with falsehood demands repair. One who desires liberty cannot forget the suffering of the other, and he is aware that on the journey to freedom, he will pass through points that will demand later purification. This understanding is not only important for the days when the Temple stands. It is the very essence of our existence as a society and a people that needs to fight for its life, and to face those who seek to wipe us out, but that still seeks to maintain its purity.

Parashat HaḤodesh

The final portion of the set of the "four *parashot*" is called "*Parashat HaḤodesh*," named for the second verse at the beginning of the chapter: "This month shall be to you the beginning of months; the opening of the year, this month will be for you" (Exodus 12:2). Why did the Sages choose this chapter in particular to be the last of the four *parashot*?

Parashat HaḤodesh is always read immediately before the beginning of the month of Nisan, to remind us of the first time that we were told of the month of Nisan, and of the Exodus from Egypt that would take place within it. Most of the verses describe the first Passover that took place in Egypt: the slaughtering of the sacrifice, the splattering of the blood on the doorposts, the laws of the holiday in that time and for generations, and more.

It is reasonable to assume that our Sages intended that the reading of these verses would remind us that Passover was approaching, and that we should begin cleaning our houses of *ḥametz* and preparing for the journey to Jerusalem to offer the Paschal sacrifice. But anyone who knows what occupies Jewish mothers in the period leading up to Passover, and the outright battle that they wage against the smallest grain of dust, as if it were the devil incarnate, will have trouble believing that there is really a need for a reminder that Passover is coming. Its approach is distinctly present in the atmosphere, in the advertisements for cleaning products, matzot, wine, and all of the other elements needed for the holiday. Why, then, did the Sages feel the need to establish that we read these verses? After all, we will all tell the story of the Exodus at length on the Seder night, when we read the Haggada. Why do we need to read these particular verses on the Shabbat before the beginning of Nisan?

Perhaps the name of the portion bears its message: "This month shall be to you the beginning of months." The days were the ones leading up to the escape from slavery to freedom. It is safe to assume that the Jewish people were very excited. Some of them, perhaps, were skeptical, and wondered whether they would really leave or not. Would the Egyptians allow them to leave? Would they feel brave enough, and have enough faith to leave? God wants to convey a foundational message before they go free: Being a slave is not just about hard work in the service of your master. The fundamental difference between a slave and a free person does not depend on the good or bad traits of the master. To be a slave is to be subject to another person's rule. One whose time is in someone else's hands, and not his own, is a slave. When the Torah states that "this month shall be to you," it is trying to tell us that, before we are set free, we need to understand that the month is meant to be for us, ours. In other words, time is meant to be something that we control. A person who does not have any formal master, but all of whose actions are determined by various obligations to time constraints that others have set for him and to which he is subjugated, is still a slave. One can be technically independent, but be subjugated to technologies that rule one's time.

It wasn't for nought that the Sages understood that this verse also teaches us of the authority of the Rabbis to determine when the new month will begin. It is well known that the Jewish month depends on the appearance of the new moon. Usually, witnesses come and testify as to when they saw the new moon, and the court determines when to begin the month based on their testimony. But the Rabbis taught that even if the judges in the court knew that a new month needs to begin, and they intentionally decided to continue the previous month, their decision still holds: "To you – even if intentional" (Rosh HaShana 25a). To be free means to be a person who rules over his own time and does not let other people determine what he will do and when. Part of this control means the power to make decisions based on an intentional mistake, and to bear the responsibility for that.

But there is yet another dimension to explore: This is the appearance of the first national mitzva in the Torah. The Torah wished to establish our calendar as a central component of our national identity, and intended for us to use the Jewish calendar as a tool to shape our consciousness. The Torah understood that a person's calendar is one of the main ways of creating a national identity and culture. This is an important challenge for us today, in modern Israel, as we live in the shadow of the secular calendar which determines most things in our lives. We can all test ourselves, whether we ask when in April Passover arrives, or on which day in Nisan the first of April comes out. If the answer to this question is obvious, we need to think about whether this is a matter of mere semantics, or whether it is a symptom of the calendar that truly determines our lives.

Shabbat HaGadol

Shabbat HaGadol, the "Great Shabbat," is the name given to the Shabbat that precedes Passover. Why was this Shabbat given this special name?

Many different explanations have been suggested. Some think that the name is connected to the fact that the rabbi delivers a great sermon before Passover on this Shabbat. Others connected the name to the *haftara* which mentions the coming of the "the great (*gadol*) and awesome day of God" (Malachi 3:23). But the most important explanation comes from long ago, in the final days of the Jewish people's sojourn in Egypt. Our Sages tell us that on the Shabbat preceding the Exodus, a great miracle occurred. What happened? The Torah relates that our forefathers were told that they were going to leave Egypt on the fifteenth of Nisan. On that night, they were told that they must slaughter a lamb, and spread its blood on the doorposts of their home, in order to distinguish between Jewish homes and Egyptian homes. They were told to take the lamb to their house on the tenth of the Nisan, which came out on Shabbat in that year. What was so special about this command? Where is the miracle in all this?

It seems that the lamb that they were asked to slaughter was seen as one of the symbols of the Egyptian cult at the time, and therefore to slaughter it was a brazen, sacrilegious act in the eyes of their Egyptian neighbors. When we add to the act of slaughter the fact that these lambs were tied to the Israelites' bedposts for four days prior, so that the Egyptians had ample time to see them waiting for slaughter, and yet, they did not intervene or protest – then what you have is a great miracle.

But I always wondered: There were so many miracles performed for our forefathers in Egypt. The ten plagues, the splitting of the sea, the fact that an entire nation went free after two hundred years of slavery. But we don't refer to any of these as a "great miracle," whereas this relatively minor occurrence (which isn't mentioned explicitly in the Torah), tying the lambs to their beds, while Egypt was silent, is referred to as a "great" (*gadol*) miracle. Isn't it strange?

It would seem that our Sages wanted to hint at a fundamental idea in religious thinking. God controls nature, and can make changes as He sees fit, for after all, who can tell the Creator of the world what to do? But there is one great principle that God established in His world: He does not want to change human beings. A person is meant to be the master of his own fate, who decides on his path in life. God will help him and more, but it is the person who must determine his path, and in the way a person chooses to go, that is how he will be led. God can perform all the miracles of Egypt, but there is one thing He does not want to do: to coerce a person's spirit. The decision to rise up against the idols of Egypt – that He leaves to a person's free choice. And here, indeed, a great miracle occurred, perhaps the greatest of all the miracles in Egypt. The children of a slave nation were willing to accept responsibility and take a dangerous step from which there was no way back. They did not know what we know. They dared to act as they did even before the plague of the firstborn, before Pharaoh and his legions drowned at sea. They were, as it were, living in the midst of the Second World War, during the years that Nazi Germany showed no signs of surrender to the Allies – and despite this, they dared to take action. This was a great miracle. The greatest of miracles. It was not performed by God, changing the natural order of the world. It took place in the spirit of the people. To be willing to publicly declare: "Yes, I belong to the Jewish people, and I deride everything that represents the Egyptian oppressors" – this is a great miracle. And to commemorate this miracle, we call the Shabbat before Passover the great Shabbat, *Shabbat HaGadol*.

Shabbat Ḥazon

The first portion in the book of Deuteronomy bears the name of the book, *Parashat Devarim*, on account of the words that Moses relates to the Jewish people before his death: long speeches, primarily words of warning and rebuke before the Jews' entry into the land, ethical directives based on the experience of forty years in the desert and hundreds of years of exile in Egypt. These speeches also contain pieces of advice from a leader who is about to depart, advice to a nation that is about to start a new life in the Promised Land. Moses mentions a number of events in his speech but puts special emphasis on the story of the establishment of a decentralized justice system composed of princes of thousands and of hundreds. These appointments were made on the suggestion of Jethro, Moses's father-in-law, based on the recognition that it was impossible for Moses to bear the burden and the disagreements of the Jewish people all by himself.

Despite the importance of this portion, the Shabbat's special name was given to it because of the *haftara* that is read following the Torah portion. There is usually a thematic connection between the Torah reading and the *haftara,* but at times the *haftara* was chosen based on the time of year that it is read, even if it doesn't have anything to do with the Torah reading. The *haftara* of *Parashat Devarim* is an example of this: the portion is always read during the days between *Shiva Asar BeTamuz* and Tisha BeAv, the period known as "*Bein HaMetzarim,*" "Between the Straits." This is the time that the nation commemorates the period from the breach of Jerusalem's walls until the destruction of the Temple, and they are considered days of danger and calamity for the Jewish people. During the three Shabbatot of this period, we read *haftara* portions that discuss the tragedies that will befall Jerusalem, and the *haftara* of *Parashat Devarim* is the most famous of them all.

The chapter that the *haftara* is taken from is found at the beginning of the book of Isaiah, which begins with the words: "The vision (*ḥazon*) of Isaiah, son of Amoz" (1:1).

This verse gives the Shabbat its name: "*Shabbat Ḥazon*," "The Shabbat of Vision." The prophecy presents Isaiah's harsh criticism of what is going on in Jerusalem in his time. He compares it to the sinful city of Sodom: "We were almost as Sodom, compared to Gomorrah" (1:9). But make no mistake, we are not talking about a modern city of sin, but a city in which many prayers were offered, as is clear from the words of the prophet: "When you pray with such verbosity, I am not listening" because "your hands, they are covered in blood" (1:15). The numerous sacrifices offered in Jerusalem are also not able to appease God, because what is demanded is to "rule justice for orphans, fight the widows' cause" (1:17). The prophet does not mince words regarding the government or the justice system, either. The corruption within these frameworks he describes thus: "Your ministers are wayward, friends to thieves, loving corruption, all of them, chasing bribes. They do not judge an orphan's case; a widow's claim does not even come before them" (1:23). The prophet does not explain why the judges do not take cases of the orphan and the widow, but it is reasonable to assume that one who is interested in receiving bribes will not receive them from the weakest strata of society, and therefore doesn't bother taking their cases. He prefers to offer his judicial services to the groups that can offer him power, money, and influence. But it could also be that the prophet is hinting that someone who is invested primarily in the pursuit of power will naturally not find the time to listen to the weak and marginalized.

The justice system that Moses established allowed for justice for all, but the danger always exists that it will forget this purpose. The cry of the prophet seems to echo from the days of destruction, through history to our very own days, calling on us to listen to the cry of the poor and destitute who need help, attention, and empathy. The name "*Shabbat Ḥazon*" might also attest to the yearning for the realization of the vision, without which "the nation becomes mutinous" (Proverbs 29:18), a vision from which can grow a world of values and ethics.

Shabbat Naḥamu

The Shabbat after Tisha BeAv is known as *Shabbat Naḥamu*. The reason is because of the special *haftara* from the book of Isaiah read on this Shabbat, which begins with the words "*Naḥamu,*" "comfort": "Comfort, comfort, My people, these are your God's words" (40:1). But there is more than a mere technical connection between the opening word of the *haftara* and the name of the Shabbat; in this case, the name of the *haftara* and its contents express the nation's yearning and longing for consolation. For the past three weeks, we have focused on our collective memories of mourning as a nation. The *haftara* portions discuss the tragedy that will befall the people in the future (which came true during our history as a nation). During the Shabbatot between *Shiva Asar BeTamuz* and Tisha BeAv, we read chapters of tragedy and rebuke that are referred to as the "Three of Calamity." Now, after Tisha BeAv, we seek to create an atmosphere of consolation, and so, the Sages established the custom to read chapters of consolation from the book of Isaiah for seven consecutive weeks. These *haftara* portions are called the "Seven of Consolation," and they accompany us until Rosh HaShana.

The first *haftara* in this series begins with a request, or a divine declaration to the Jewish people: "Comfort, comfort, My people." Why did the prophet choose to repeat the word "comfort"? Wouldn't once have been enough? Moreover, can emotions be programmed? Can a button be pushed that says: "Comfort"?! Can days of mourning and days of comfort be established in advance?

In general, there is something very strange about the Jewish calendar. It has joyous days, like the holidays of Sukkot, Passover, Purim, and on the other hand, it has days of mourning, like the days "Between the Straits," and Tisha BeAv, and then these are followed by days of comfort. It is reminiscent of an orator who has notes written next to the text that he delivers: "Now it is time to cry" or "Now it is time to dance." Can days of mourning, consolation, and joy be decided by a formula? Are these merely artificial rituals, or is there a deeper phenomenon here that demands our inspection?

Moreover, we can understand what joy is, and what mourning is, but what is the nature of days of consolation? Are these days of restrained joy, or perhaps softened mourning, or perhaps a completely different emotional dynamic? Many people feel a kind of lightening after Tisha BeAv passes. Vacation trips increase dramatically, including among those who are not meticulous about the strictures of Jewish law. There is a sense of ease in the air. Is this what consolation is?

The central question here is: What is consolation? How does it affect us? How are we meant to heed the call of the prophet: "Comfort, comfort, My people"? It seems that the Sages' enactment to read verses of consolation until the end of the year does not only come to offer a response to the sense of mourning and despair that comes from the destruction of the Temple. We do not find that the Sages prescribe special practices during these days that are connected in any way to destruction and consolation. There seems, rather, to be an attempt at understanding a person's spirit on the personal, familial, and communal levels, that needs occasional periods of encouragement and renewal, with a spirit of consolation, perhaps specifically at the end of the year, during the preparations for the new year.

When the Midrash comes to tell the story of our *haftara*, it presents the following question: "Comfort,

comfort, My people" – who is meant to be comforting whom? Is God calling on someone to comfort His people, or is God asking His nation to comfort Him for the loss of His creations? The Midrash not only presents the rhetorical question, it also presents a parable, comparing the events of the destruction of the Temple to a man who became a widower. Is it not obligatory to console the husband who lost his wife? The meaning is clear: God is, as it were, the bereft husband (*Midrash Eikha Zuta*, Buber edition, version 2, chapter 1). What is this midrash seeking to teach us?

The story of consolation would seem to be connected to the original description of the world deteriorating because of the actions of men who corrupt it. God expresses His great pain at what has occurred, and perhaps even at creation itself. He did not desire to create a world that was corrupt and rotten. Until one man, Noah, overturns the regret and the pain and gives creation new meaning. This is the first time that consolation is mentioned in Scripture: "This one will bring us comfort after all our labor and the sorrow of our hands" (Genesis 5:29). Every person experiences pain and regret over things that he has ruined in his life. This can cause despair and crushing frustration. This is the place for consolation, which seeks to tell a person that despite what was corrupted along the way, there is comfort and there is hope. Human beings are capable of repair. Therefore, a period of consolation will always come at the end of the year, to deepen our sense of confidence in our ability to begin anew in the coming year. Perhaps this is the meaning of the phrase "to suffer twice over, and to be consoled twice over," and this is the reason for the repetition "Comfort, comfort." Sadness is not just about the pain of destruction, but also our lack of faith in our ability to rebuild anew. Consolation is also twofold, because it offers us the confidence in our ability to rebuild, as well as the sense that destruction can be a tool for new rebuilding.

The fonts used in this book are from the Arno family

Maggid Books
The best of contemporary Jewish thought from
Koren Publishers Jerusalem Ltd.